Dakhleh Oasis Project: Monograph 10

Vernacular Mud Brick Architecture in the Dakhleh Oasis, Egypt

and the Design of the Dakhleh Training and Archaeological Conservation Centre

Frontispiece El-Qasr, Tomb of a Saint and attached mosque

Dakhleh Oasis Project: Monograph 10

Vernacular Mud Brick Architecture in the Dakhleh Oasis, Egypt

and the Design of the Dakhleh Training and Archaeological Conservation Centre

by

Wolf Schijns

with contributions by

Olaf Kaper and Joris Kila

editorial committee

A.J. Mills, C.A. Hope, C.S. Churcher, I. Gardner

Oxbow Books

The Monographs of the Dakhleh Oasis Project

First published in the United Kingdom in 2008. Reprinted in 2018 by
OXBOW BOOKS
The Old Music Hall, 106–108 Cowley Road, Oxford OX4 1JE

and in the United States by
OXBOW BOOKS
1950 Lawrence Road, Havertown, PA 19083

Dakhleh Oasis Project Monographs

Paperback Edition: ISBN 978-1-84217-059-5
Digital Edition: ISBN 978-1-78297-546-5

A CIP record for this book is available from the British Library

For a complete list of Oxbow titles, please contact:

UNITED KINGDOM
Oxbow Books
Telephone (01865) 241249, Fax (01865) 794449
Email: oxbow@oxbowbooks.com
www.oxbowbooks.com

UNITED STATES OF AMERICA
Oxbow Books
Telephone (800) 791-9354, Fax (610) 853-9146
Email: queries@casemateacademic.com
www.casemateacademic.com/oxbow

Oxbow Books is part of the Casemate Group

Contents

List of Illustrations

Preface

This study was carried out as preparation for the design and construction of an archaeological working and training centre in the Dakhleh Oasis in Egypt. It contains a description of the mud brick architecture in the oasis, based on a field trip carried out in 1997 by Wolf Schijns (architect), Margriet Schijns (architect), Olaf E. Kaper (Egyptologist) and Joris D. Kila (art historian).

The finished text of this report was compiled by three authors, each with their individual speciality, as follows: the introductory survey of the medium of mud brick in architecture was compiled by Joris Kila. The geographical and historical chapters are written by Olaf E. Kaper, member of the Dakhleh Oasis Project, and the field observations and their interpretations are compiled by Wolf Schijns, who also prepared the drawings for this section. The final text of the report is the result of modifications and additions made by the three authors together. The photographic illustrations were all made during the 1997 field trip.

We are very grateful to A. J. Mills for his assistance in the field and for reading through the manuscript, and to David Brown of Oxbow Books for accepting the report for publication. Margriet Schijns prepared the drawings for figures 34, 48, 53, 58 and 66.

Finally we would like to thank the Netherlands Embassy in Cairo for the financial support that made part of this research possible.

Chapter 1
Introduction to the Project

1.1 - The D.O.T.A.C.P.

In 1994 the idea was born to erect a training centre for the inhabitants of the Dakhleh Oasis where interested members of the local population would be offered education and training in various archaeological disciplines. This initiative was to be implemented by scholars participating in the Dakhleh Oasis Project (D.O.P.).

The D.O.P. has been active since its establishment in 1977. Its aim is to study the relationship between environmental change and human activity. A major component of this research is the study of human cultural development in the Dakhleh Oasis since earliest times up to the present. Apart from specialized archaeologists from various backgrounds, the team comprises members from several supporting disciplines, such as conservation, architecture and drawing.

The D.O.P. carried out a comprehensive archaeological survey of the entire oasis between 1978 and 1982, as a result of which detailed knowledge became available on the history of the oasis. Following the survey, a number of specific sites were chosen for excavation and related activities, such as conservation. The local population was involved in these excavations from the start, and it appeared that a genuine interest developed among them. This same group of people has been enthusiastically enlisted to participate in the yearly excavations. The idea of an organized training scheme was born as a result of their enthusiasm.

The training project has now been running since 1996. It is entirely carried out by the staff of the D.O.P. A class room and conservation centre had to be designed and built for its purposes which will be described in detail below. The name of this project is the Dakhleh Oasis Training and Archaeological Conservation Project (D.O.T.A.C.P.).

The aim of the D.O.T.A.C.P. can be summarized as the transfer of knowledge from the foreign experts of the Dakhleh Oasis Project to selected inhabitants of the Dakhleh Oasis, in the fields of the history, archaeology, architecture, material culture, and the natural history relating to the human presence in the Dakhleh Oasis. The teaching program serves as a means to create a greater understanding and appreciation of the region's heritage and respect for its cultural remains, as well as for its natural surroundings and landscape. The program will strengthen the local sense of cultural identity, and will bring about an increased appreciation in cultural matters among the local oasis population.

The D.O.T.A.C.P. is supported by the Dakhleh and Farafra Pharaonic and Roman Inspectorate of the Supreme Council of Antiquities in Mût. The implementation of the project involves the active participation of this office, which has shown keen interest in the project. They assist in selecting trainees (students) and they will further employ the trainees for their excavations and restoration projects in the oasis. The Dakhleh and Farafra Inspectorate acts as the Egyptian counterpart for the D.O.T.A.C.P. project.

1.2 - The need for a D.O.T.A.C.P. Centre

In accordance with the plans outlined above, the D.O.T.A.C.P. included the building of a centre for classroom and laboratory training. The combination of indoor training with training in the field is central to the comprehensive "hands-on" education of the project. The topics to be covered include the cultural history of the region with an emphasis both on material culture, the natural history, art history, architecture, and anthropology of the Dakhleh Oasis. The regular participants in the D.O.P. act as the project's instructors, contributing their individual academic or technical expertise. They provide teaching of excavation techniques and various kinds of recording techniques, such as drawing, surveying, keeping a field notebook, and elementary photography skills. The course is primarily intended to be practical, aiming at people without an extensive educational background. The education is innovative in character, in that it concerns knowledge and expertise that are currently not available in the region.

The widely different nature of the sites under study by the D.O.P. ensures a large variety of topics to be incorporated in the curriculum. Different historical periods will be presented by studies of the sites from the Pharaonic, Roman, early Byzantine and medieval Islamic periods and also from Palaeolithic and Neolithic eras. The sites range in type from cemeteries, settlements, and campsites to temples, all of which lie within the concession area of the D.O.P. granted yearly by the Supreme Council of Antiquities.

Practical aspects of dealing with antiquities will be taught in the laboratory including elementary conservation methods. The practical courses that are envisaged indoors include the following, listed in random order: the handling of fragile artefacts, preparation of elementary object descriptions, storage of antiquities, manual cleaning of metal objects, storing data utilizing computers, recording of data on object cards, the technology of studio photography and darkroom facilities, aspects of technical drawing and of pottery restoration.

A progressive specialization in one or more of these fields will be encouraged for those trainees who show a distinct ability to perform the tasks involved with skill and some degree of independence.

I.3 - Designing and building the centre

The chosen location of the D.O.T.A.C.P. training centre lies central in the oasis only a few kilometres west of its capital, Mût. The site consists of a large hill, a so-called "spring-mound" (ancient spring), on which there are no archaeological remains.

The design of the Centre was sponsored and executed by the University of Technology at Eindhoven (the Netherlands), which also directed the present study of local building traditions in the oasis. The architectural study was seen as a necessary basis for the design of the building, because it was to be made according to the distinct local traditions in mud brick vernacular. Despite the still lively traditions in mud brick architecture of the Dakhleh Oasis today, its forms and building techniques have never before been the subject of systematic study. The centre had to be built in local materials and involving the local builders in the hope that the erection of a large building in the local vernacular would encourage local pride in this type of architecture. As elsewhere, the local vernacular is slowly being superseded in the oasis by the more recent building forms and techniques in reinforced concrete and concrete block while building in mudbrick becomes associated with low social status.

The building costs of the centre, including its design, were borne largely by the Local Cultural Fund of the Netherlands Embassy in Cairo, which also funded the start of the training programme itself. The land was donated by the Governorate of the New Valley, and cosponsors were the Dakhleh Oasis Project, the University of Technology, Eindhoven, and the Leiden University Fund. The plans and the finished building are further described in chapter V below.

Figure 1. Street in Bashendi

Figure 2. Mud brick making on the building site of the centre

Chapter II
Geographical and Historical Background

II.1 - The geography of the Dakhleh Oasis

The Dakhleh Oasis lies in the Western Desert of Egypt, about 500 km due south-west of Cairo. The term oasis is Egyptian in origin (Leclant 1993). It was coined especially to designate the depressions in the surface of the Western Desert. The Dakhleh Oasis consists of a relatively large depression in the desert surface, roughly 80 km from east to west, in which the subterranean artesian waters can easily be tapped and the clay desert surface is a fertile ground for agriculture.

The Western Desert is among the most arid regions on earth, and rainfall is all but nonexistent. The subterranean waters are found at 300 to 400 m below the surface, but the modern wells drilled by the government go as deep as 1000 m or more. This water is warm, varying between 24° and 40° C. Throughout its history, Dakhleh has cultivated the following products: dates, grapes (partly used for wine-making), olives, jujubes, grain, wheat, rice, madder, fruits and vegetables. In addition, there were mines of alum in the oasis.

In the north, the depression is bordered by a steep escarpment of about 500 m which dominates the landscape. In the south the surface rises gradually until it reaches the same height. The total area of the oasis depression measures c. 1600 km^2, but the surface which is actually under cultivation covers only a small part of this, even less than half its size. In fact, the typical oasis landscape shows the cultivated land everywhere interrupted by stretches of desert.

There are two kinds of water sources in the oasis. One is the spring (*ayn*) which is basically a deep hole in the ground, the other is the drilled well (*bi'r*). Normally, the water is brought to the surface by the natural artesian pressure which also causes the water to fill the canals and to flood the land. A large well often serves several farmers at the same time, in which case a wooden device for dividing the water is installed at the mouth of the well, called a *khashaba* (Hivernel 1996, 108-08, figure 31). In order to irrigate larger plots of land in the oasis the use of water lifting devices is necessary, such as the *sâqiya* or water wheel, which is powered by one or two cows.[1] The manpowered *shâdûf* is used specifically for small plots of land. Nowadays, only a few wells in the western end of the oasis can make use of the natural water pressure. The

1 On this device, cf. Menassa, Laferrière, *La saqia: technique et vocabulaire de la roue à eau ègyptienne*, Cairo 1974. For Dakhleh: cf. Hivernel 1996, 106-07, figure 29.

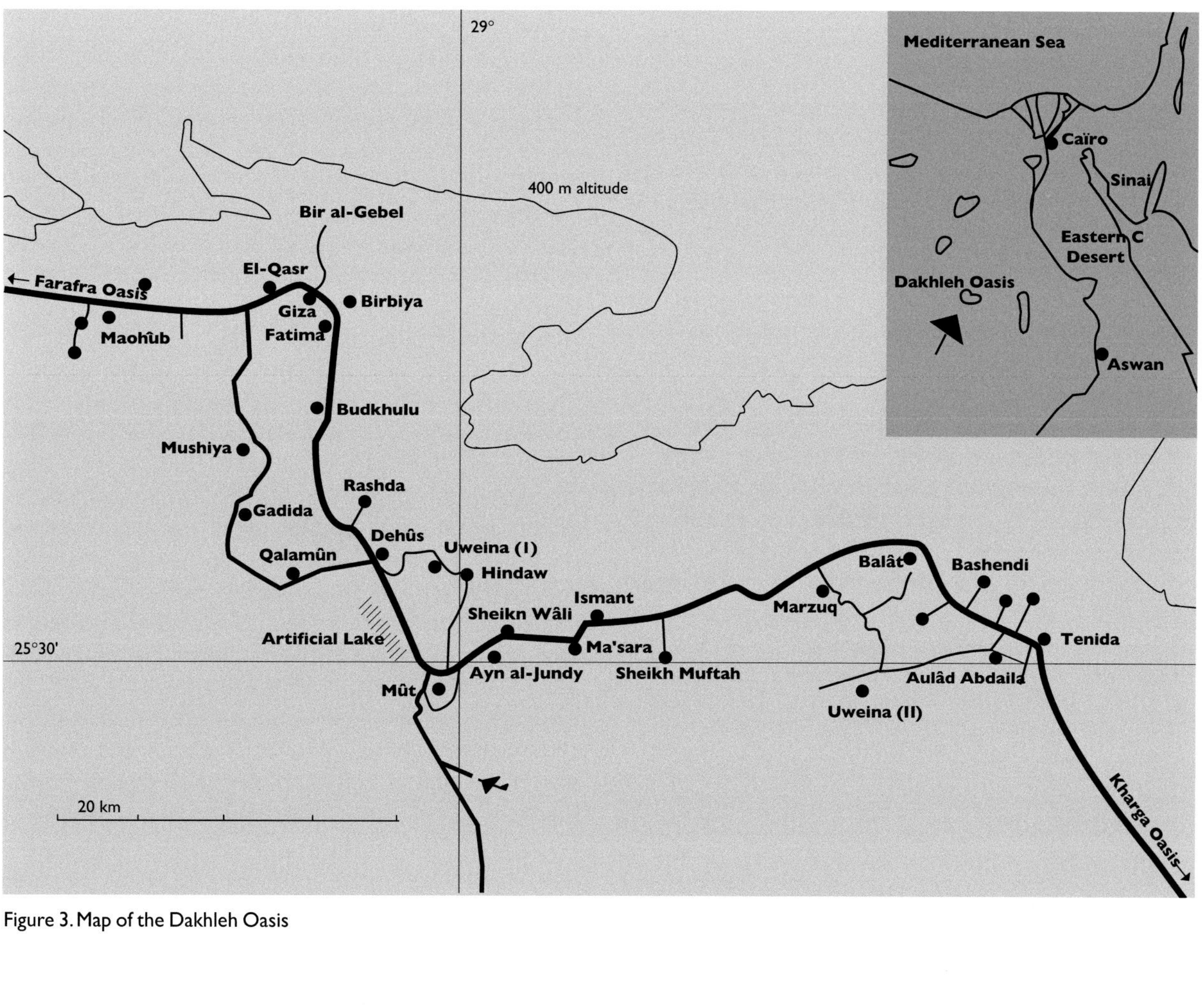

Figure 3. Map of the Dakhleh Oasis

large number of new government-installed wells in the oasis has lowered the water table, so that the new wells draw their water from a depth of up to 1000 m. with the use of diesel pumps.

There are twelve historical villages in the oasis: Tenida, Balât, Ismant, Ma'sara, Mût, Hindaw, Rashda, Qalamûn, Gedida, Mushîya, Budkhulu and El-Qasr. These villages existed well before 1900.[2]

In addition to these ancient villages, one can find a large number of more recent villages, which are designated with the name of *ezba* (pl. *ezab*). These *ezab* were mainly, though not all, established after 1900 when the government undertook action against the marauding bedouins in the area which used to make village life very insecure. The older villages had, in order to be defensible, walls of mud brick surrounding them on all sides. The village of Ismant preserves part of such a defensive wall. After the area was made safe a great number of hamlets were established closer to the fields that were used as winter habitats for the inhabitants of the larger villages (Hivernel 1996, 62, 104-05). They were occupied during the periods of most intensive agricultural activity in Dakhleh, between November and July.

Examples of such *ezab* in Dakhleh are: Bashendi, Uweina, Marzûq, Sheikh Muftah, Sheikh Wâlî, Giza, Birbiya and Fatima (the latter three are known collectively as the *ezab* of El-Qasr) and Maohûb. The phenomenon of the *ezba* however is much older, and the same division in settlements can also be observed in Roman Dakhleh. Around the Roman town of Ismant El-Kharab (ancient Kellis) a large number of hamlets functioned that were designated as *hydreuma*, water points.

During the course of the twentieth century, people have tended to return from the *ezba* to their ancestral villages less and less frequently, and many houses in the old villages have been abandoned as a result. At the same time, the former *ezab* have become villages in their own right. According to Hivernel, this can be partly ascribed to the increase in the material possessions of the inhabitants, accompanied by the advent of electricity to the region in the eighties (Hivernel 1996, 188). The increase in household appliances made the traditional pattern of a biannual relocation of the household simply too cumbersome an affair. However, the same phenomenon was observed in Dakhleh already in the early forties (Mitwalli 1943, 301).

Apart from houses in the village and *ezba*, a typical family possesses one or more *hush*, i.e. a walled stable and storage space or pen, which also serves as a general storage space that is usually erected close to the village or close to the farmer's land.

The natural conditions and the way of life have not changed much in the oasis since antiquity. The inhabitants of Dakhleh still adhere to a pattern of existence which was established for the area many ages ago. The harsh conditions of the hyper-arid environment of the Western Desert have imposed a way of life adapted to such conditions. Streets in the village are often covered against the sun, and each house is divided into separate living quarters for summer or winter to accommodate the markedly different temperatures of the seasons.

II.2 - A Brief History of the Dakhleh Oasis

The history of Dakhleh can be traced back to the remotest antiquity. The work carried out by the Dakhleh Oasis Project since 1978 has added considerably to our knowledge of the oasis. The earliest traces of human habitation in Dakhleh can be dated back to 250,000 BP, when the oasis was still largely covered by lakes, which have helped to shape the landscape of the oasis. Throughout the Eastern Sahara man lived as hunter-gatherer, and the water in places such as Dakhleh led to fertile hunting areas.

The Ninth Millennium bp saw the emergence of a group of inhabitants in Dakhleh with a different culture, which is referred to as the Masara unit. These people inhabited an oasis that had occasional rainfall, but in which the lakes had largely dried up. The stone tools of this population are of complex manufacture, and they rarely produced simple types of pottery. Later in the Neolithic two further units can be distinguished in the archaeology of the oasis, respectively termed the Bashendi and the Sheikh Muftah units. These are dated to the period between 8000 and 4200 bp when giraffes, ostrich, and antelope were found in abundance.

This situation would change dramatically as a result of the development of a centralized state in the Nile Valley. During the later part of the Old Kingdom, probably during the Fifth Dynasty (c. 2400 BCE), officials from the Nile Valley arrived in Dakhleh with the aim of colonizing the region. The reason for their interest was the trade routes through the Sahara and into Nubia that were intensively used at that time. Old Kingdom pottery is found along these routes at Abu Ballas (cf. Sers 1994, 198-207). Dakhleh seems to have been the only inhabited oasis at this time as there is yet only slight evidence for settlements in the Kharga Oasis. Probably as a result of the influx of the Egyptians the local culture of the Neolithic peoples of Dakhleh disappeared without a trace. Henceforth, Egyptian gods were worshipped in the local temples, and Egyptian style ceramics were manufactured in the workshops.

2 They appear upon the map of Dakhleh produced by the Survey of Egypt in 1900, reproduced in Wagner 1987, plates.

During the succeeding Pharaonic dynasties, the oasis would remain under Egyptian control. The archaeological evidence from different periods of Egyptian history shows that the oasis remained inhabited, albeit on a small scale, and that its culture remained essentially Egyptian in nature. The French excavations at the town of Ayn Asîl and the cemeteries at Kila ed-Dabba (Balât) have yielded material mainly from the late Old Kingdom and many succeeding periods, whereas the survey and excavations of the Dakhleh Oasis Project have provided material from this and all other periods.

A noticeable increase in archaeological remains can be observed from the 26th dynasty (c. 600 BCE) onwards. The population gradually increased until in the Roman period the population had again reached high levels: new villages, farmhouses and temples were built throughout the oasis in a second wave of large-scale colonization of the area by the Egyptians from the Nile Valley. About half of the archaeological sites currently known in Dakhleh date from this time. Of these, the site of Ismant el-Kharab, ancient Kellis, has been under excavation since 1986.[3] This is a town that dates back to the Ptolemeic period whose houses and other buildings lie buried beneath several metres of wind-blown sand (cf. Hope in Bagnall 1997, 11-15). Its buildings bear witness to highly sophisticated building techniques in mud brick. Vaulted roofs were extensively used with some vaults spanning a width of nearly five metres. In total, twenty ancient temples from this period have been identified in the oasis, fourteen of which were constructed in mudbrick. These temples were destined for the pagan cults of the old pharaonic religion. In addition, several churches have been found which may be ascribed to either Christian or Manichean inhabitants of the oasis in the third and fourth centuries CE. Other churches in the oasis, such as Deir Abu Matta and Deir el-Molouk, were constructed during the Sixth Century.

3 Work largely funded by the Australian Research Council and Monash University.

During the first centuries after the Muslim conquest of Egypt, the sources suggest that several attempts were made at achieving independence for the oasis. Its inhabitants around this time were counted among the Lawata ethnic group, which has Berber origins. Dakhleh was more important than Kharga at this time, as is evident from the place of residence of the chief administrator of Dakhleh and Kharga, which was set up in the villages of Qalamûn and El-Qasr.

In 950/51 and again in 955 CE, Nubian raids on the oasis from the south caused much destruction. Later, in 1026 an epidemic of smallpox decimated the population. The arrival of members of the Banu-Hilâl tribe made up the numbers of the population again. The desert trade routes were used intensively, linking the oasis to Cyrenaica, the Maghreb, Cairo, and the Hijâz. The most important commodity exported by Dakhleh at this time was indigo.

It is reported that a part of the population still adhere to the Christian religion during the tenth century, after which the significance of this religion declined. The episcopal sees of Dakhleh were probably abolished already

Figure 4. Old El-Qasr

Figure 5. Mud brick masonry at El-Qasr

Figure 6. Interior view of the restored "House of Abu Nofri" at El-Qasr

during the 13th and 14th centuries. However, the presence of a painted cross on the lintel of the access doorway to one of the small streets in El-Qasr attests to the survival of the Christian faith in the oasis into the 17th century at least.

A Turkish military presence in Dakhleh can be demonstrated by the wooden door lintels, which are inscribed with the names of the house owner (Figure 16). Several Turkish names have been preserved on the lintels in the villages of Balat, Ismant, Qalamûn and El-Qasr (Décobert & Gril 1981). The Arab historian Al-Idrîsî reported that the Kharga Oasis had been deserted during the 12th century, and that the situation in Dakhleh had deteriorated as well. From 1320 onwards, the slave trade provided a new stimulus for the ancient trade routes to the south, the Darb El-Arba'în, from which Dakhleh profited too by selling its agricultural produce to the large caravans. This profitable situation lasted until 1874, when the Darfûr area was annexed by Egypt, after which, in 1880, the slave trade was banned by the British authorities. In the early twentieth century, the prosperity of the oasis increased again slightly. Under British rule, a hospital was built in Mût.

The Sanûsi, a religious movement that operated from the Kufra Oasis in Libya, gained a foothold in Dakhleh in the early years of the century, and in 1916, their leader Sayyid Ahmed el-Sherîf even attempted to set himself up in Dakhleh when he had to flee Kufra. He arrived in the oasis with a small bodyguard, but he was soon defeated by the British military authorities (Evans-Pritchard 1949, 128-9). The power of the movement was broken only in 1931 when Kufra was taken by troops of the Italian government, and a group of some 500 people fled the oasis in an attempt to reach Egypt (Almásy 1997, 201-09). The popularity of the movement left its traces in Dakhleh, for instance in the male name Sanûsi which is still popular today.

In 1959, the New Valley Project was initiated, aiming principally to enhance the economic development of the Kharga Oasis. Large numbers of Egyptians moved from the Nile Valley to Kharga, some also went to Dakhleh. Dakhleh became part of a new governorate under the name of the New Valley which also includes Kharga and Farafra Oases, whereas previously it had been under the Governorate of Assiut. Under the new arrangement, Mût became the capital of the *Markaz* of Dakhleh.

Systematic archaeological exploration of the Dakhleh Oasis was first taken in hand by the Egyptian archaeologist Ahmed Fakhry at the end of the sixties and the beginning of the seventies. His principal discovery in the area was the Old Kingdom necropolis and settlement near Balât. In 1977, the French Archaeological Institute in Cairo (IFAO) took over the excavations at these sites, and the rest of the oasis was awarded in concession to the Canadian Dakhleh Oasis Project in 1978. The latter project has continued working until today under the direction of A.J. Mills, with the aim of studying the history of human habitation in Dakhleh in all its aspects, as described in the introduction above.

II.3 - A brief history of mud brick architecture

More than one third of the world's population lives in houses made of unfired earth bricks or stamped earth, materials also known as mudbrick, *adobe*, *terre crue*, *pisé*, or rammed earth (Woodforde 1976). The important historical link of this material with the country of Egypt is clear from the fact that the term most often used for the bricks, *adobe* (from the Spanish), as also the Arabic *tûba*, has its roots in the Coptic language and ultimately in the ancient Egyptian term *ḏbt* (Vycichl 1983, 210-11).

The oldest known sun-dried mud bricks date back at least 10,000 years, namely the bricks found deep in excavated sections of ancient Jericho. They have the appearance of long loaves of bread in which the maker has sometimes left patterns of thumb impressions which are intended to improve the adhesion of the bricks to the mud mortar (Woodforde 1976). Today, modern mud brick houses are still being built in the town of Jericho and there are even plans to reintroduce the ancient mud brick production- and construction methods in the area. In Egypt the material is also still in use and in some cases, such as in New Gourna, similar attempts have been made to recreate the ancient techniques or even improve on them.

Figure 7. A brickmaker in Bashendi

Sun-dried bricks were so effective that kiln-fired bricks did not appear until the third millennium BCE, long after baked pottery had shown the effect of high temperatures on clay. A major step forward in the methods of mud brick production was the use of box moulds to replace the moulding by hand, which happened around 3000 BCE. The famous walls of Jericho date from the beginning of this period and they were largely built of box-moulded mud bricks in the form of large even slabs. Their regularity made it possible to utilize thinner mortar joints.

In Egypt all architecture built before c. 2700 BCE was for the larger part constructed of mud brick. At this point the step pyramid of pharaoh Djoser was built at Saqqara by the architect Imhotep, and was the first building composed entirely of stone blocks. The question arises if this change to ashlar masonry was caused by a desire for durability, or for reasons of status, or a combination of both. Archaeological investigation of ancient mud bricks is facilitated by the fact that the organic components mixed into the mudbricks can be dated fairly exactly by using the ^{14}C dating technique. In Egypt, dating is more commonly based on the analysis of the associated pottery finds from the same locus, because the dating by ceramics from pharaonic Egypt yields more exact results.

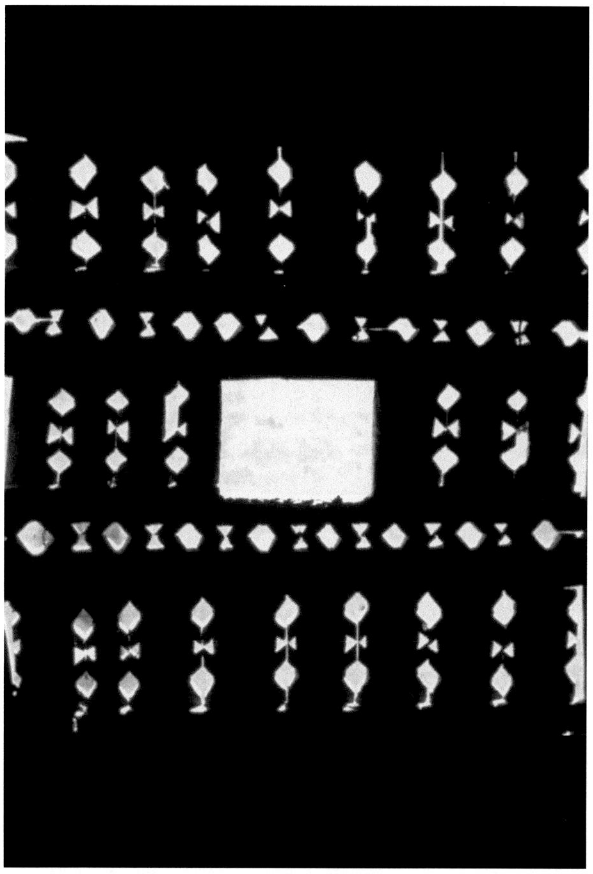

Figure 8. A traditional window grating at El-Qasr

The ancient Egyptian mud brick production techniques are well known. The methods are referred to in texts, such as the Old Testament (Ex 1:14), and several representations of the manufacturing process have been preserved in murals. In addition, the methods employed by contemporary Egyptians are still virtually unchanged (Figure 7). On the basis of these sources, the production process in pharaonic times can be summarized as follows (cf. Clarke and Engelbach 1990): The brick maker, in Arabic *tawwâb*, first locates a sediment of Nile mud suitable for brick fabrication. His assistants dig up the mud and throw it in a hole in the ground (*ma'gana*). The wet substance is then mixed with sand, straw or chaff (whatever is available) utilizing a hoe (*fâs*) and the feet of an assistant. The addition of chopped straw or sand throughout the alluvial Nile mud, which is by itself already of a high plasticity, will prevent the bricks from cracking during the drying period. The assistant then takes a round or oval mat (*bursh*) plaited of strips of palm leaves fitted with handles on either end, and he places as much of the mixture as possible onto the *bursh*. In this way, it is easier to transport the material to the brickmaker who puts some of the substance in a wooden rectangular mould which is open on two sides. He scrapes off the surplus of clay from the top with his hand, before lifting the mould. The freshly moulded brick remains on the ground on a layer of sand and straw, while it dries. This procedure is repeated until the whole area is covered with neatly arranged rows of bricks only separated by the thickness of the mould's edge.

An average brickmaker in modern Egypt is capable of producing c. 1000 bricks per day. The bricks are left to dry for three days before they are turned and left to dry until the end of the week when they are strong enough to be stacked in piles. The pure Nile mud shrinks c. 30% during the drying process. Studies of the traditional village architecture in the Nile Valley are by Eigner (1984), who studied a number of villages in the eastern delta and near Luxor, and by Henein (1988), who studied a village close to the town of Akhmim.

Evidence of an early use of mudbrick construction has been found in many other parts of the world. Apart from the Near East it has been found, for instance, in Central and South America, in China, India, Africa, and Turkey. In Turkey archaeologists have found the remains of mud brick houses built before 5700 BCE using large slabs. Adobe was used in the Chicama Valley of Peru at c. 300 BCE, the bricks being shaped in bamboo moulds. Apparently, mud brick making was invented at least twice; once in the Old World and once in the New.

In Greece, mud bricks were utilized in the fourth century BCE. Later the bricks were also used in Rome. Vitruvius Pollio, in his treatise on architecture, written about 25 BCE discusses the sun-dried bricks and the aspects to be considered when making them. Adobe was and still is an extremely suitable medium to be used in the building of cheap housing facilities. Its low cost has made it an attractive possibility also for developing countries today.

History shows that through the ages the material was not only used for houses but also for more prestigious buildings like ziggurats (ancient Mesopotamia), pyramids (ancient Egypt), palaces (ancient Egypt), mosques, churches (e.g. Faras in Nubia) and fortifications (parts of the Great Wall in China, and the Second Cataract forts in Nubia). The fact that large parts of some of these ancient buildings have remained intact proves the potential sustainability and durability of earthen architecture. The most remarkable remaining building in this respect is the so-called Shunet ez-Zebib in Abydos, Egypt. This is a mudbrick enclosure, measuring 65 x 122 m, and 5.5 m in thickness, which is still standing in places up to 11 m in height. This enclosure was constructed for King Khasekhemui of the 2nd Dynasty, at c. 2740 BCE. Of course, prestigious mud-brick buildings were constructed with extreme care, but the supposed fragility of unfired bricks can thus be shown to have no basis in fact.

II.4 - An introduction to Hassan Fathy and his work in the Oasis

The Egyptian architect Hassan Fathy (1900-1989) became famous for his ideas on how to realize low cost housing for the poor in a responsible manner, considering both hygiene and efficiency, using mud as his building material. His ideas are put forward in his most popular book: *Architecture for the Poor: An Experiment in Rural Egypt* (1973). This work describes the New Gourna Village project (1946), where the architect attempted to involve the future inhabitants of the new village he was creating in the building process.

Fathy's work shows that form and application in architecture in some communities may have strong roots in century-old customs and traditions. The local conditions are important factors influencing the architect's design, and these do not let themselves be changed in the name of progress, as Fathy found out when the local population of Gourna, who were also the future inhabitants of the new village, refused to cooperate with him. One of the problems for the locals was Fathy's use of domes. They did not want to live under domed mudbrick roofs as these were specifically associated with funerary architecture. This Egyptian case study has clearly demonstrated the need for careful study and interpretation of the architectural and cultural history of an area before introducing a major building project.

At present, there is again a small Egyptian renaissance of indigenous building techniques and of traditional materials like mud brick. This is particularly apparent in the Fayûm where architect and Fathy follower Adel Fahmy has trained a number of village masons to construct domes and vaults in mud brick. A "new" housing trend was thus created in this region mainly for artists, intellectuals and a small part of the local population (cf. *Egypt Today* August 1994). There is in fact a need for more research on the subject so that the medium can be adapted to modern needs and be practical for wider parts of the population. There are recent threats to mudbrick architecture which have to be addressed, such as chemical pollution and modern large-scale and intensive irrigation projects. The old problems associated with this type of architecture still persist, notably the threats of erosion, warfare, and the generally inferior status attached to mud brick buildings in society.

The first building Hassan Fathy erected in the Kharga Oasis was the Baume-Marpent Enterprise Resthouse in 1959. In 1963 Fathy was asked by the Administration of Desert Development to participate in the planning of an agricultural community 60 kilometres south of the capital of Kharga Oasis at Baris (Steele 1988). This centre had to accommodate 250 families and it should also serve a series of new villages around it. The settlement was to be called New Baris Village. While designing New Baris, Fathy focussed on the climatological problems that had to be overcome and he studied the indigenous village architec-

Figure 9. White washed mud brick house at Qalamûn

ture of the region. He was much inspired by the ruins of el-Bagawat, an ancient pagan and Christian cemetery in the Kharga Oasis dating from the third and fourth centuries CE, which was built entirely of mud brick. The tombs of Bagawat are elaborate structures, with lime plastering and painting, pilasters, domes and various types of vaulting (Grossmann 1989).

Fathy also copied the traditional village layout and the indigenous techniques of the New Valley in order to cope with the high temperatures (with max. 48° C in the shade) which are normal for this area during the summer months. He laid out the streets in a north-south direction so the houses would remain in the shade for most of the day. The public buildings projected in the centre of New Baris were equipped with interior courtyards like the Arab villages of the past (Fathy 1989). As weapons in the battle against the heat he used the shade and the traditional *malkaf*, a wind catch on the roof opening towards the north.

Unfortunately building activities at New Baris were stopped in 1967 only one year before the village was to be finished, due to the war with Israel. This would not be the end of Fathy's interest in the oases, however. In 1970, he built a co-operative centre in Kharga, the Hotel Rubat in Kharga City and a hospital in Mushîya, Dakhleh. Buildings in Mût and the village of Maohûb were designed by Hassan Fathy and a tourist village currently under construction in Mût is also ascribed to him.

Chapter III
Description of the Mud Brick Architecture of Dakhleh

III.1 - A history of the study of mud brick architecture in the oasis

The mud brick architecture of the oases in the Western Desert has long been featured in discussions by Egyptologists on the topic of architectural types of houses in ancient Egypt. It is interesting that only the Kharga Oasis has been mentioned in these discussions, simply because Kharga was the only oasis which was occasionally visited by scholars from the early years of the twentieth century onwards. This was made possible by the construction of a rail link connecting Kharga with the Nile Valley.

It is generally assumed that the modern village house architecture is the direct descendant of the ancient Egyptian types (Eigner 1984, 2). Norman de G. Davies (1865-1941) in his discussion of the ancient Egyptian town house which appeared in 1929, was the first to point at the parallel to the ancient house forms found in Kharga. Davies was acquainted with the oases because of his epigraphic work for the Metropolitan Museum of Art, New York, at the temple of Hibis in Kharga. Davies noted the correspondences between the appearance of some ancient house drawings and the modern houses in the town of Kharga (1929, p. 246). Elsewhere (p. 250), he points at "the fortress-like towers that can be seen in ruins on the plain of the Great Oasis", as a useful parallel to ancient house models which often depict houses with several storeys. These observations were again cited in an American exhibition catalogue of 1982 (*Egypt's Golden Age*, p.35). The German Egyptologist Herbert Ricke (1901-1976) pointed out the occurrence of rooftop structures on the houses in Kharga in a publication in 1932 as parallels for the assumed presence of such structures at Amarna (Ricke 1932, p. 33, n. 1).

The traditional houses of Kharga City have all but disappeared today, but the villages of Dakhleh still preserve many comparable structures, even though these have been completely ignored in the study of ancient pharaonic housing. Herbert Winlock (1884-1950) visited Dakhleh in 1908 and he remarked, for instance, on the occurrence of "palm-leaf wattled fences around the tops of houses" in the village of Ismant, (as in Figure 27), which he had also observed in Kharga.[4] Otherwise, Winlock did not dwell on the possible pharaonic antecedents of the houses he described, but he did provide some interesting observations and photographs in his travelogue (1936), which indicate that the houses in Dakhleh were not much different from those in Kharga.

Moreover, we learn from Winlock's descriptions that, unlike Kharga, the villages in Dakhleh have not changed much since 1908. In Balât, for instance, he noticed a white-washed house decorated with red horizontal bands containing Arabic calligraphy, which is identical to the decorations still found in the villages today. His photos of the villages of Tenida and Qalamûn (Winlock, pl. 8) confirm the unchanged appearance of these villages over the last 90 years. Other elements, of course, have been subject to changes in fashion, such as the use of decorative brick-work in the upper storeys of the houses, in which bricks in the colours red and white are laid in a checker pattern (illustrated Winlock, pl. 31). Winlock observed this feature regularly in 1908, in the villages of Balât, Ismant, Hindaw, Uweina, Budkhulu, Gedida, and Qalamûn,[5] whereas it is remarkably absent in the villages today.

4 Winlock 1936, p. 22. This particular feature is discussed by Davies in the article cited, and depicted in his figure 5.

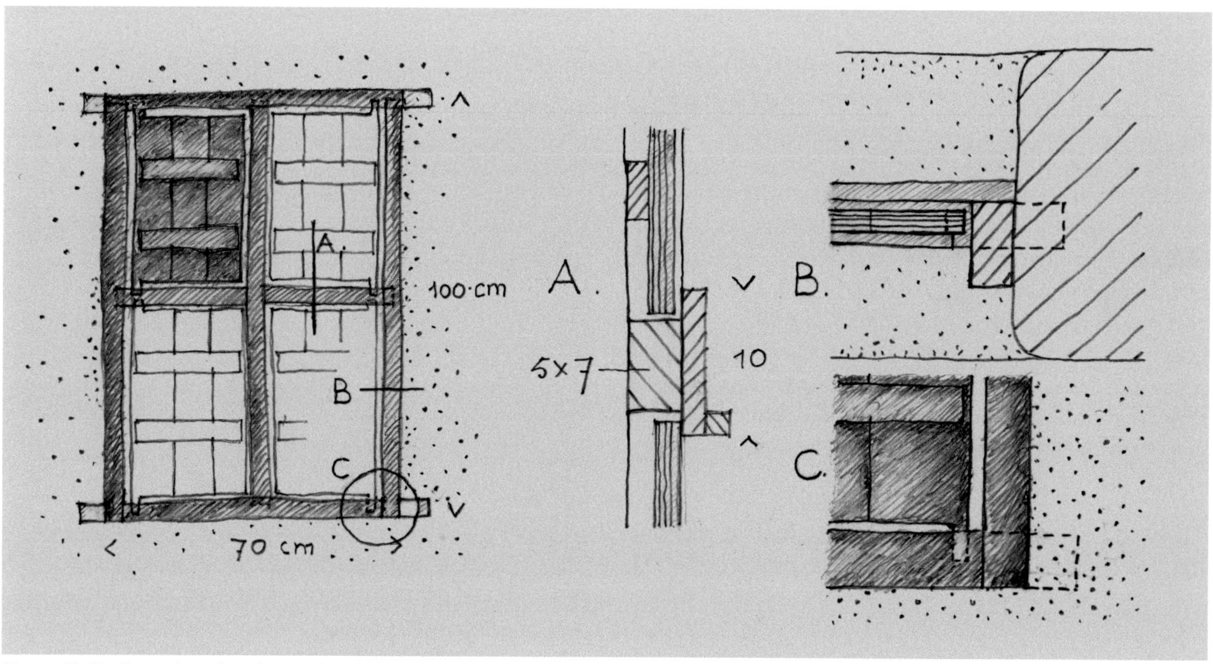

Figure 10. Traditional window frame observed in old Mût

For the present study, the following villages were visited in 1997: Balât, Mût, Hindaw, Qalamûn, and El-Qasr, as well as the *ezab* of Bashendi, Uweina, and Marzûq. A small number of houses selected at random of which plans and elevations were drawn up. Of other houses only remarkable details were recorded in drawing.

One example of an architectural element which we noted to have remained unchanged for at least two millennia is a particular type of window frame which recurs in the houses of several villages in the oasis (Figure 10). The window frame in question is divided into four compartments by crossed wooden mullions, each of which can be closed independently with a wooden shutter opening inwards. During the day, the upper sections of the window could be left open to catch some light and air, whereas the lower section would only be opened in cooler conditions at night. In the cold winter months, the window could also be closed entirely. This exact type of window has been found in excavations of houses in the Fayûm, at the Roman period town sites of Karanis and Dimeh (Ricke 1966, p. 122-23), and the same window type is depicted on stone models of houses from the same time, or perhaps earlier.[6]

III.2 - The distribution of the ancient settlements in the oasis

The fortified villages are usually built on top of small hills known among geologists as "spring mounds". Formerly, these villages possessed a full defensive wall system, formed by the blind rear walls of the houses which stand along the perimeter of the village (Figures 11-15). The entrances to the village were formed by one or more gates (*fatha*). The purpose of these fortifications was to offer protection against attacks by Berbers or other Bedouin groups.

Since the end of the last century, the security of the villages has become guaranteed by a larger government and police presence, and this has led to a new kind of settlement being formed. The ancient villages were from now on only used during the hot summer season, whereas in all other periods the farming population moved closer to the fields, into temporary structures which were grouped into hamlets, the so-called *ezab*. The village of Balât engendered no less than 30 of such *ezab*, which were located at a distance of up to 15 km. During the course of time, the *ezbas* have acquired a permanent character. In fact, it has become more difficult for the families to keep

Figure 11. Qalamûn. Old aerial view
(aerial photograph taken in c. 1965 at 1 km)

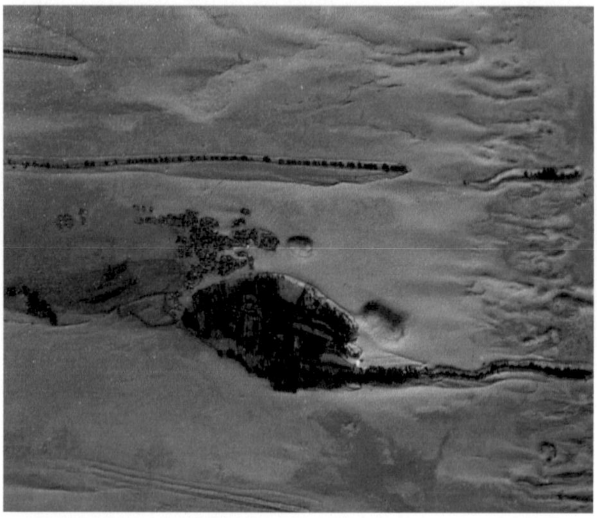

Figure 12. Bashendi. Old aerial view
(aerial photograph taken in c. 1965 at 1 km)

Figure 13. El-Qasr. Old aerial view
(aerial photograph taken in c. 1965 at 1 km)

5 Winlock 1936, pp. 18, 22, 23, 24, 37, 39. Note that at Gedida "many of the houses are built of red and white brick" (p. 37), whereas at Mût, Winlock observes that there were none at all (p. 41).

6 Egypt's Golden Age (exhibition catlogue, Boston 1982), p. 34-35, nos. 1-2; Petrie 1886, pl. 18.3.

Figure 14. Balât. Old aerial view
(aerial photograph taken in c. 1965 at 1 km)

Figure 15. Mût. Old aerial view
(aerial photograph taken in c. 1965 at 1 km)

moving house, owing to, among other factors, the increase in material possessions in recent times (cf. the discussion in the introduction, above).

III.3 - The urban fabric

The contrast between the two forms of settlement in the oasis is reflected in the different structure of their respective urban fabric. The ancient villages have developed in a concentric manner, whereas the *ezbas* have a more regular perpendicular plan. The ancient villages of Qasr, Balât, Mût, and Qalamûn were built using the model of a concentric fortress with a dense build-up and narrow, often covered streets (*shâri'*) or alleys (*zuqâq*). In the labyrinth of streets one can distinguish concentric and radial connecting streets, which allow the internal spatial communications within the village to take place.

The ancient village consists of a system of neighbourhoods which function as relatively independent units within the village structure. The houses within such a unit can be accessed through semi-public alleys (*darb*), which lie behind a large gate (Figure 17). These alleys mark the transition from the secluded space of the home to the public street. The *darb* is inhabited by an extended family, usually of one lineage. A variant form exists, called a *hâra*, in which a number of different families share an alley as an autonomous community.

The façade of the *darb* is usually decorated (see below), and its gate has a wooden lintel with carved inscriptions and decorations relating to its inhabitants (Figure 16). These doors formerly were closed during the night.

In recent times, the houses in the *darbs* have sometimes been regrouped and the ancient fortified walls around the village have been breached so that new houses could be added to the outer walls of the village. As a consequence, the closed aspect of the ancient village has been fundamentally altered.

The village of Bashendi developed out of a former *ezba* belonging to Balât. It is already mentioned by Drovetti in 1819 (in Jomard 1821, 101). The village is immediately surrounded by fields and gardens. In contrast to Balât, the houses in Bashendi are more spacious and the streets are wider too. Often the houses have been built back-to-back instead of being grouped around a *darb*. There still are some houses belonging to the same family, which have been built around a central court (Figure 54).

The traditional village architecture reflects some general rules of urban planning based on tradition. For example, the uniform height of the buildings prevents one house from casting a shadow over another house. The privacy of the household is ensured by shielding the private quarters against unwanted curiosity. Special wooden windows, imitating the *mashrabiya* type, make sure that the members of the household cannot be observed from the street or from the neighbouring houses.

The streets and alleys do not follow a rigid plan, but they reflect the individual character of the houses and their time-honoured divisions and fusions within the village walls. Extending the first floor of a building across the street is permitted, provided one does not cause ill-effect to anybody or hinder the free flow of traffic below. The houses display an organic pattern of growth and development which is quite in keeping with their organic building material.

Figure 16. Lintel with carved inscription at El-Qasr

Figure 17. Entrance to the *darb* at Balât

III.4 - Typology of buildings in the ancient villages

The fortified village in Dakhleh developed from a mediaeval centre on top of a hill outwards to the bottom of the hill and onto the plains below. The recent extensions of new housing and public buildings are situated on the plain. The ancient centre on the hill, the buildings of which are now invariably in ruins, contained the public utilities, such as a *madrasa* (El-Qasr), an oil press, and a mosque. In Balât, the village contains two ancient water sources within its confines. It is noticeable that there never was a need for open spaces such as a market square in the ancient centres.

Following the implementation of the New Valley Project in 1959, new administrative centres were created outside the villages comprising the likes of a village council, schools, a post office, or a telephone exchange. The increasing traffic over the newly built asphalt roads caused new houses to be erected along this road, and coffee houses, as is the case in El-Qasr and Balât. In general, the arrangement contrasts with the layout of the typical village in the Nile Valley, where the public buildings are located in the village centre and the domestic buildings are found extending in all directions around them.

The houses form the principal element in the village architecture of the Dakhleh Oasis. They are compact, with a closed outer face (Figure 18). The layout of the individual houses is similar: their plans are generally based on adjoining plots of land measuring about 5-6 m. in width. The upper storey of the houses is of equal width or smaller, unless it extends over a street below. Only the lower part of the house is plastered on the outside and sometimes it is also whitewashed; the upper storey displays the fabric of its brickwork. The internal layout of the larger houses is determined by the specific needs of the members of the extended family. The traditional houses were built for families consisting of a patriarch with his married sons and their families. The architecture of the house takes into account, for instance, the need for separate rooms for male and female users of the house, rooms for guests, or areas for specific use during the winter or summer. The actual dimensions of the rooms are partly determined by the limited span width of the wooden roofing beams, which are of palm or acacia.

Apart from a pragmatic description, one may give a symbolic interpretation of the structure of the house, which refers to the nature of family life and its social structure. Thus, the houses may be described as concentrically built, with the cooking place (*kanûn*, cf. Figure 66) as their centre. The basic kitchen is an important place, but at the same time it is the most intimate sector, because it is reserved for the women. The other rooms are grouped around it, with the guests' reception room (*maq'ad*) as the most

Figure 18.The closed outer face of the houses on the edge of the ancient village of Balât

Figure 19. Balât. Roof terraces in the centre

Figure 20. Balât.A house extension over a street

public and most peripherally placed room. This trajectory from interior to exterior expresses the transition from the intimate to the public and from the familiar to the strange. The rooms closest to the house's heart are actually dimly lit and small, whereas the exterior rooms closer to the street are larger and receive more light.

III.5 - The traditional building techniques

The use of modern materials, such as reinforced concrete, concrete blocks, steel beams, and shaved wood, can be observed in modern buildings in the oasis mainly outside the heart of the ancient villages. The traditional architecture, still practised up to the present day, uses materials that are found in the immediate surroundings of the village. These are sun-dried mud bricks and mud mortar for the walls, logs of acacia or palm wood and palm ribs, palm rope and palm leaves for the roofing, acacia wood for the doors and windows, and sometimes stone for flooring and lime plaster for a whitewash. The general use of these materials is one of the reasons for the relative unity in appearance of the ancient villages. Variety occurs only in the size of the houses, for instance, houses may be larger in some villages than in others. The houses in El-Qasr, a former capital of the oasis, are notably larger in scale than the contemporary houses in Qalamûn for instance (Figures 19-20).

Figure 21. House in El-Qasr

Figure 22. Houses in the ancient centre at El-Qasr

Figure 23. Interior with decorative brickwork

Figure 24. Outside decorative brickwork at El-Qasr

Figure 25. Entrance façade at El-Qasr

Figure 26. Garden fences at Hindaw

Figure 27. Houses with characferistic roof fences at Balât

The finish of the bricks may also vary. In general, walls are constructed of unburned bricks of 21 x 12 x 7 cm, but variants occur of a larger size. The bricks are made in wooden moulds from a mixture of clay, sand, chopped straw, and water.

The laying of the bricks is done with a clay and sand mortar. The outer walls are laid in double rows (*tubtên*, lit. "two bricks"), measuring 40-50 cm in thickness. Such walls are capable of carrying weight and they contain the heat. Walls of upper storeys and interior walls are laid in rows of one brick-and-a-half (tûba *w^{a}nuss*) in thickness. The most commonly encountered pattern of bricklaying alternates one layer of stretchers with one layer of headers (Figure 5). An older pattern using headers exclusively was found in combination with monumental entrance façades or window frames with arches as well as with other types of decorative bricklaying.

Fences around the gardens are usually constructed of palm branches tied together and cemented at the bottom with mud (Figure 26). The same technique is applied in constructing fences around the roof terrace (Figure 27). Foundations are shallow and laid in mud bricks on solid earth. In case the level of the public space outside rises as a result of garbage deposition and natural dust accumulation, the floor of the house may come to lie lower than the street level. For this reason a few houses have steps

Figure 28. Street in Bashendi

Figure 29. A house entrance below street level in Bashendi

Figure 30. Tombs at the cemetery in Hindaw

Figure 31. Interior of the mosque at Uweina with a remarkable roof construction

leading down from outside (Figure 29). In recent times, foundations are also laid in dry stone, up to a height slightly above ground level.

Vaults used to be common in the houses in Dakhleh in Roman times, but in recent construction they are only found employed in the domes of tombs or in the conical top of a minaret (Figures 30, 41). This type of dome construction presents problems for the transition to the square shaped walls below, which is solved by the use of squinches or flat wooden supports. The current most common roofing construction employs rough wooden beams of acacia (ø c. 15 cm), or palm logs that have been split into segments, usually halves.

The beams are laid at about 60 cm distance. The usual length of these beams is most often between 3.5 - 4.0 m, and never longer. In larger spaces, such as the mosque at Uweina (II), rafters are used supported by earth columns (Figure 31). Upon the beams, a layer of palm ribs stripped of their leaves is positioned at right angles to the beams. The ribs are tied together with ropes, and sometimes, a decorative wickerwork of palm ribs is visible from below which assists in keeping the ribs in place. The layer of palm ribs is then covered with a layer of palm leaves and finally a layer of mud or bricks, with a smooth finish.

Above wall openings such as windows and doors, the weight of the mud bricks is supported by composite wooden lintels which may extend into the adjacent masonry, or even over several windows at once. In many places, the lower part of the opening has been plastered in a round shape, conjuring up the peculiar image of an inverted arch (Figures 32-34).

The staircases have acquired this rounded aspect too, partly as a result of prolonged use and repeated plastering. The front of the steps has been reinforced with wood or a palm rib (Figure 68). The staircase as a whole is supported by a slanting floor supported by round casuarina wooden beams, below which there is a storage space (*hânût*). On the roof terrace, there are additional storage facilities erected around the stair well. These take the form of tall oval bins made of clay, used for the storage of food (Figure 35). They are closed with a flat cover made of clay, and when the bin has been completely filled up, the remaining openings may be closed with clay.

The doors are clamped into place, and they are made to turn on a pivot post set in the lintel and the threshold. The door can be locked with a characteristic wooden lock (Figure 38). Window frames are made in various shapes. An often encountered type has wooden crossed mullions with four identical wooden shutters, mentioned above, which allows varying degrees of ventilation in the house. No glass panes have been observed. Other means of air

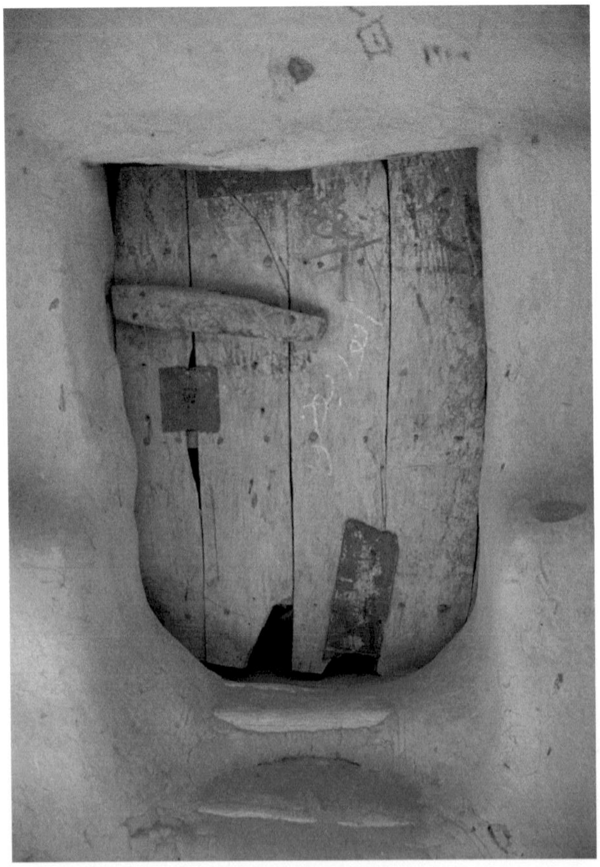

Figure 32. Front door of a house in Balât (p.42)

Figure 33. Window opening plastered in a round shape

Figure 34. Support for a water jug between staircase and an interior door at Bashendi (p.33)

Figure 35. Storage bins on the staircase in Balât

Figure 36. The Kaaba, datail of a decorated house façade in Bashendi

Figure 37. Koranic inscriptions an a white washed house façade in Bashendi

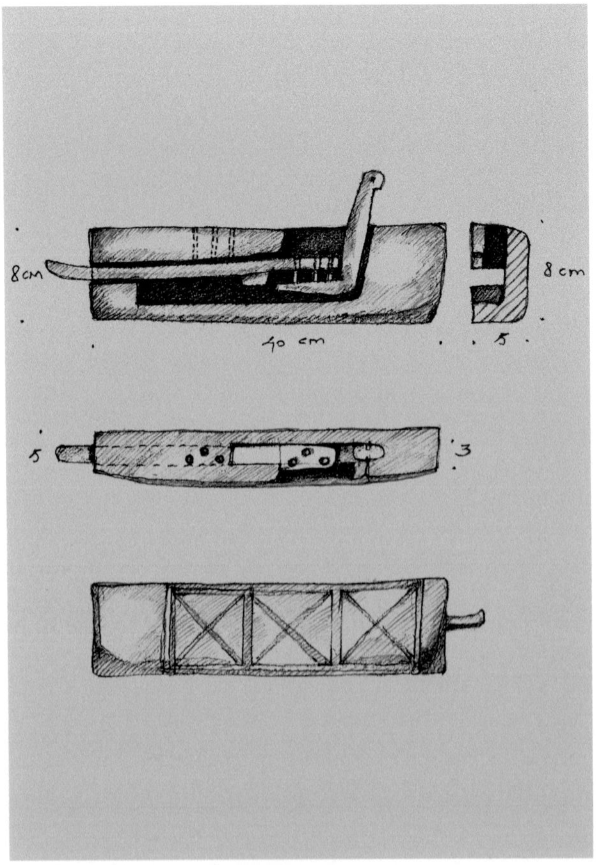

Figure 38. Wooden lock and pintle hinge

Figure 39. Front door with lock in Bashendi (p.33)

conditioning take the form of a wooden grating (Figure 8) or of openings or slits in the masonry. Also, the half-open kitchen roof and the stair well take care of the cross ventilation of the house. The kitchen roof is opened to allow the smoke of the stove to escape.

Toilets are located in the upper storey, with a compost room below. This type of "dry toilet" is also found in House I of our documentation in Bashendi, where the toilet appears to have a more public function, because it opens onto the street.

The finishing of the exterior masonry generally is a combination of bare masonry with plastered masonry, sometimes with an added whitewash and even painted decoration. This combination makes for a varied appearance of the streets. The mud plaster on the walls is applied using the hands. The first layer consists of a mixture of clay, sand, and chopped straw. On top of this comes a smooth finishing layer of fine clay and sand which has to be regularly maintained. Some walls receive an entire or partial whitewash, on which paintings are sometimes applied. Horizontal bands with Koranic inscriptions are found both outside and inside the houses, and a testimony of a pilgrimage to Mecca may be painted on the façade, with pictorial elements such as a car, an aeroplane, the Great Mosque at Mecca, the Kaaba, etc., usually depicted in bright colours (Figure 37).

Figure 40. Minaret of the mosque at Qalamûn.

Figure 41. El-Qasr. Minaret behind the tomb of a Saint

Figure 42. Uweina (II), a pencil shaped minaret

III.6 - Mudbrick Minarets of the Dakhleh Oasis

An interesting feature of the oases' architecture is the mudbrick mosque, because these are often the only non-modern large public buildings to be seen in the villages. Of special interest are the minarets of these mosques, because they show some of the influences on the architecture of the oasis (Figures 40-43). Their architectural styles show both correspondences and differences with Mamlûk stone architecture. The minaret of the village of Uweina (II) (Figure 42) resembles the minaret of the old mosque in the oasis of Marzûq in southern Libya. (Richter 1960, 78). Both are variants of the Ottoman minaret type, with its characteristic pencil-shape. Perhaps the medium of mudbrick gave rise to a preference for a rounded top on the Ottoman minaret type.

Another feature was noted on the corner of a house at El-Qasr, which resembles a feature well-known from Fatimid architecture, called the *muqarnas*, the honey-comb-shaped carved decoration of vaulted roofs or entrances, also found inside domes and especially on the squinches, the transitional zones between the round dome and the square space below it. In El-Qasr, a comparable decorative pattern is rendered in mudbrick at the transition from a rounded corner of a house to a straight corner above (Figure 24).

Figure 43. El-Qasr. Minarets in the ancient city

Chapter IV
Case Studies of Houses

IV.1 - House 1 in Bashendi

This house is situated at the edge of a series of regular rectangular lots in the south of Bashendi (Figure 44). Each lot measures more than six metres in width, and the present house occupies two of these lots. It is the property of the family of Amar Sayed, whose grandfather was said to have built it some 90 years ago. The house (Figure 46) has been divided into separate spaces for the male and female members of the household. On the ground floor this becomes apparent in the location of the living room (*saqîfa*) and the guests' reception room (*maq'ad*) immediately behind the house façade. Behind these rooms lie the women's quarters, centred around the kitchen patio. A separate staircase leads from here to the roof terrace, which in winter is mainly used by the women, and where also the food is stored. The sleeping rooms are located on the first floor.

The traditional domain of the men is located in the front of the house. From the living room a staircase leads to the first floor which is used as living room during the hot summer months. Various draughty corners of the house are used for placing water jars (Figure 48), which are thus refrigerated by the wind. This house also has a special support (*rekîza*) for a water jar added at the bottom of the stairs inside the living room (Figure 34).

The walls of the house have been built of mud bricks measuring 21 x 12 x 7 cm, with a thickness of the outer walls of 42 cm. Mud plaster has been applied both inside and out, whereas the outside also shows parts of the masonry. Painted Arabic calligraphy in the living room attests to the pilgrimage made by the owner of the house. Next to the house entrance, the façade has been decorated with a pictorial testimony of the pilgrimage to Mekka (Figure 47).

As all mud brick requires regular maintenance, the house is repaired twice yearly. The clay for plastering is chosen for its colour. In this household, the clay employed is called "white clay". As a result of this regular plastering and other repairs carried out on the wall, floors, ceilings, stairs, niches, and fixed furniture, the appearance of the architecture changes over time. All originally straight lines become more rounded, by which the modelling and the movements of the human (female) hand becomes apparent. The mud floors in the house, as well as the mud brick benches (*mastabas*) are swept and covered with clean sand of a reddish colour once every week.

The roofs in this house are supported by rough beams of acacia, of which the length does not exceed 2.50 m. The ceiling of palm ribs has been plastered together with the beams, creating an impression of waves.

The doorways are surmounted by lintels of wood (*khashab*), in which the door pivot is set as well. The windows have no frames or shutters. Some former windows have been bricked, whereas the remaining window openings have not been fitted with any woodwork.

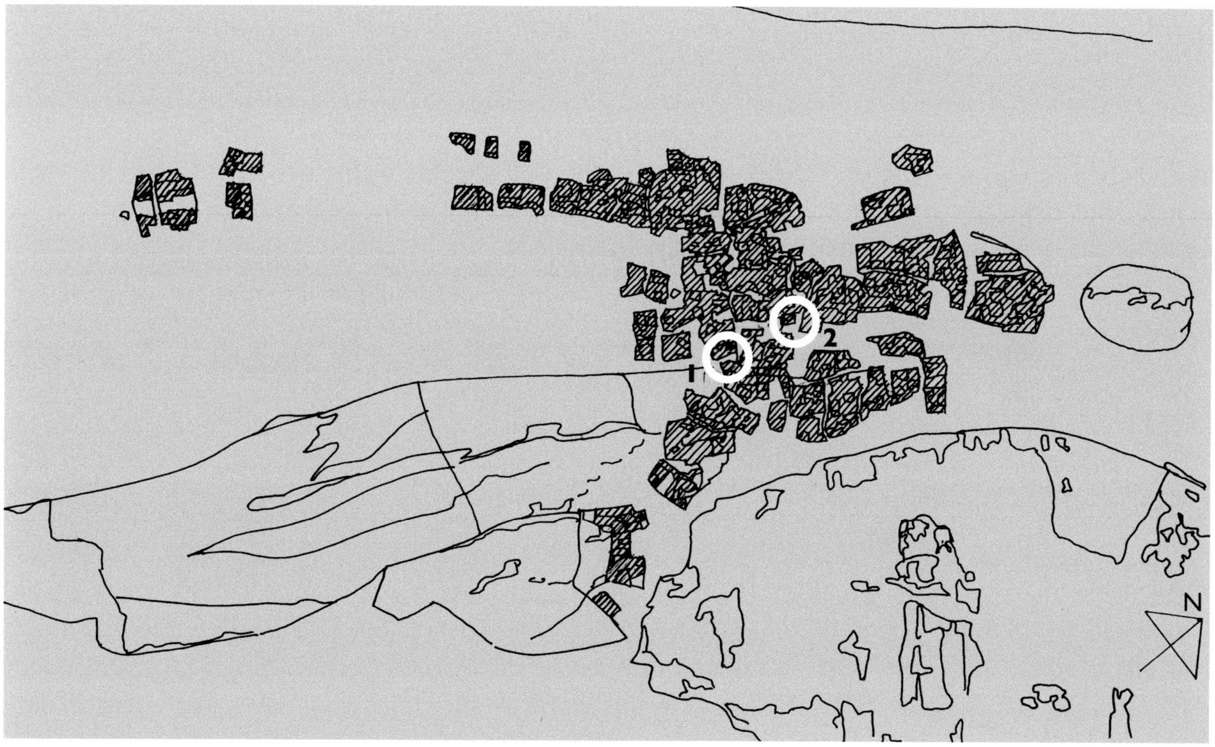

Figure 44. Schematic plan of Bashendi, with the location of houses 1 and 2

Figure 45. Bashendi. View at the village, seen from the top of a spring mound

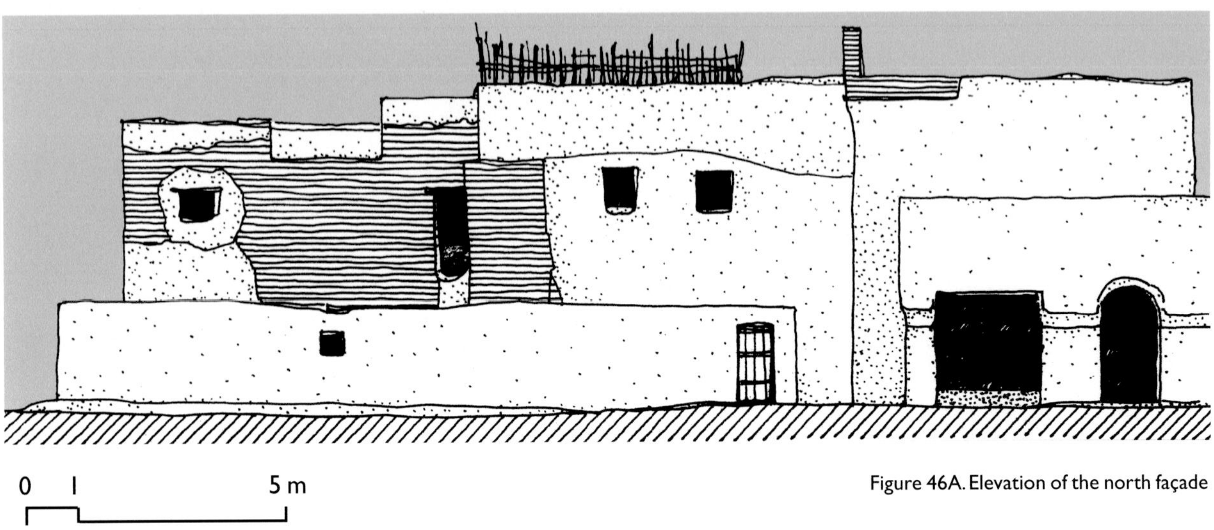

Figure 46A. Elevation of the north façade

Figure 46. House I in Bashendi, plans and elevations

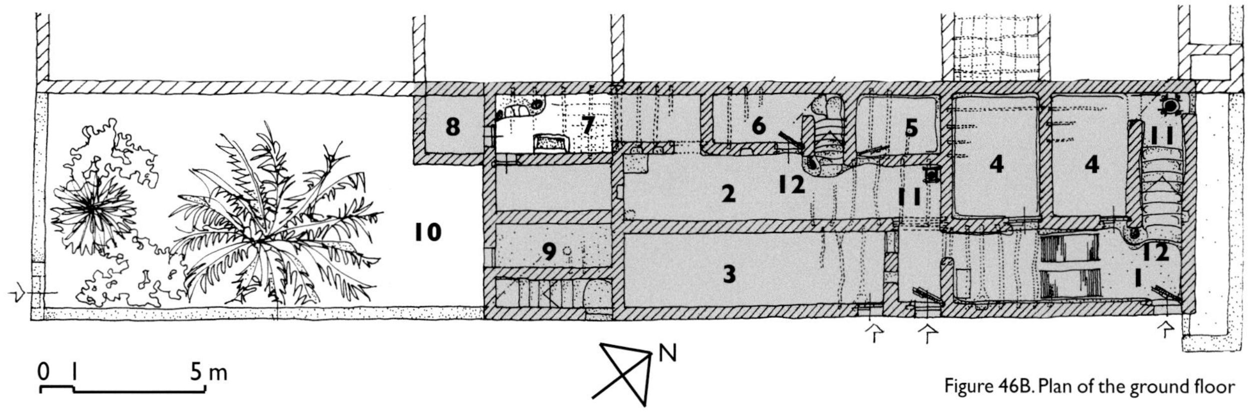

Figure 46B. Plan of the ground floor

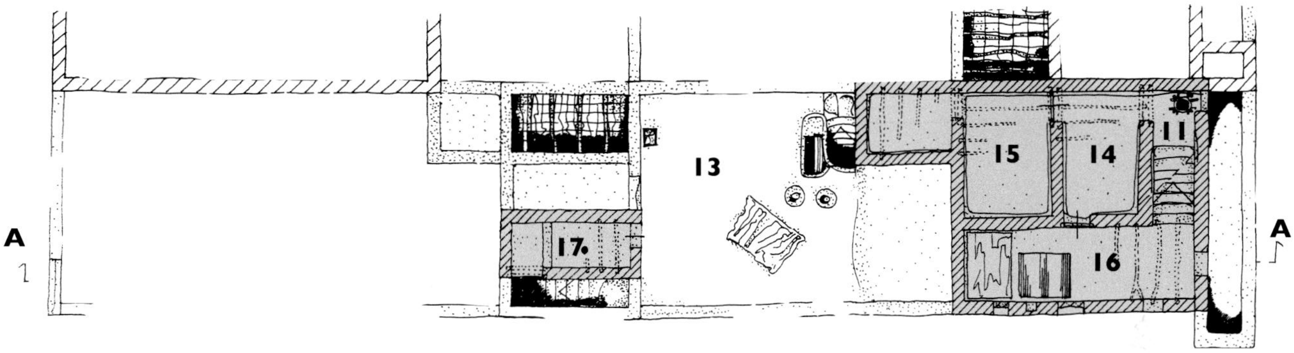

Figure 46C. Plan of the first floor

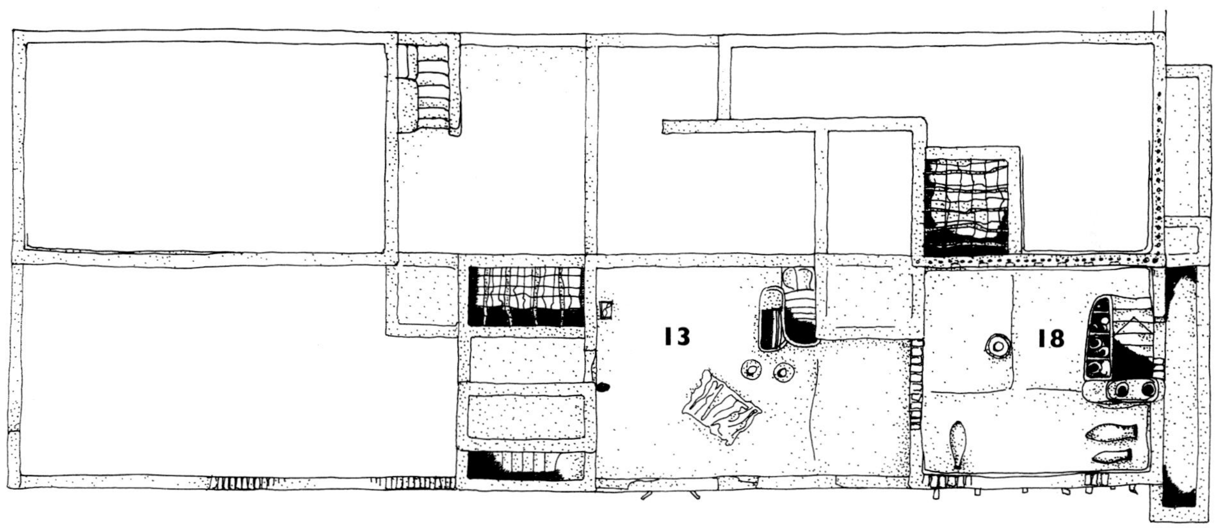

Figure 46D. Plan of the roof terrace

1. Entrance way / reception room / living room (*saqîfa*)
2. Hall (*shari'a*), and reception room for the women
3. Guests' reception room (*maq'ad*)
4. Store (*makhzan*)
5. Bathroom (*hammâm*)
6. Bedroom
7. Kitchen (*matbakh*)
8. Chicken pen (*katakît*)
9. Compost room toilet
10. Garden
11. Water jar on a stand
12. Support for a water jar (*rekîza*)
13. Roof terrace
14. Corridor
15. Bedroom / store
16. Upstairs living room (*mijlis*)
17. Dry toilet
18. Roof terrace

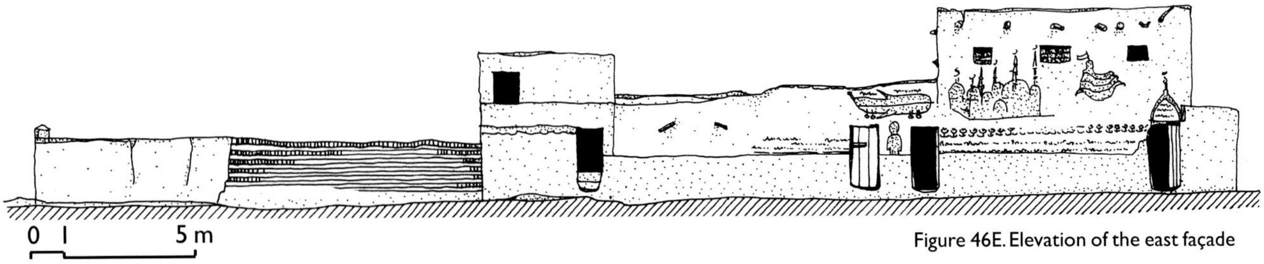

Figure 46E. Elevation of the east façade

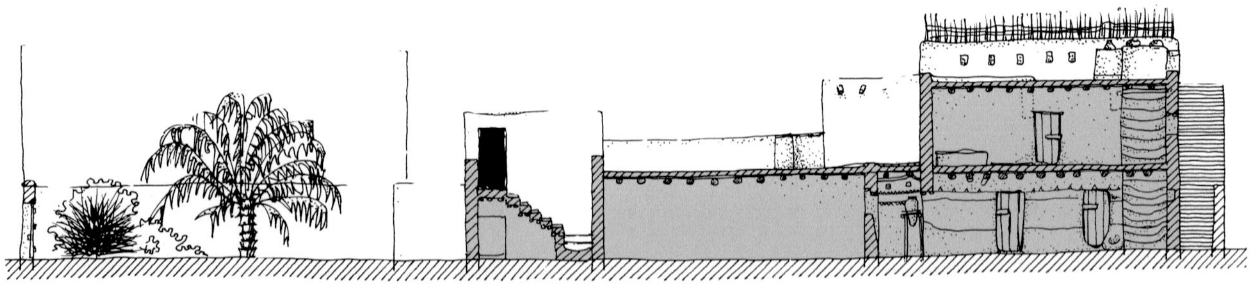

Figure 46F. Section north-south (A-A)

Figure 47. House 1, East façade with decorations of a pilgrimage to Mecca

Figure 48. Water jar inside house 1

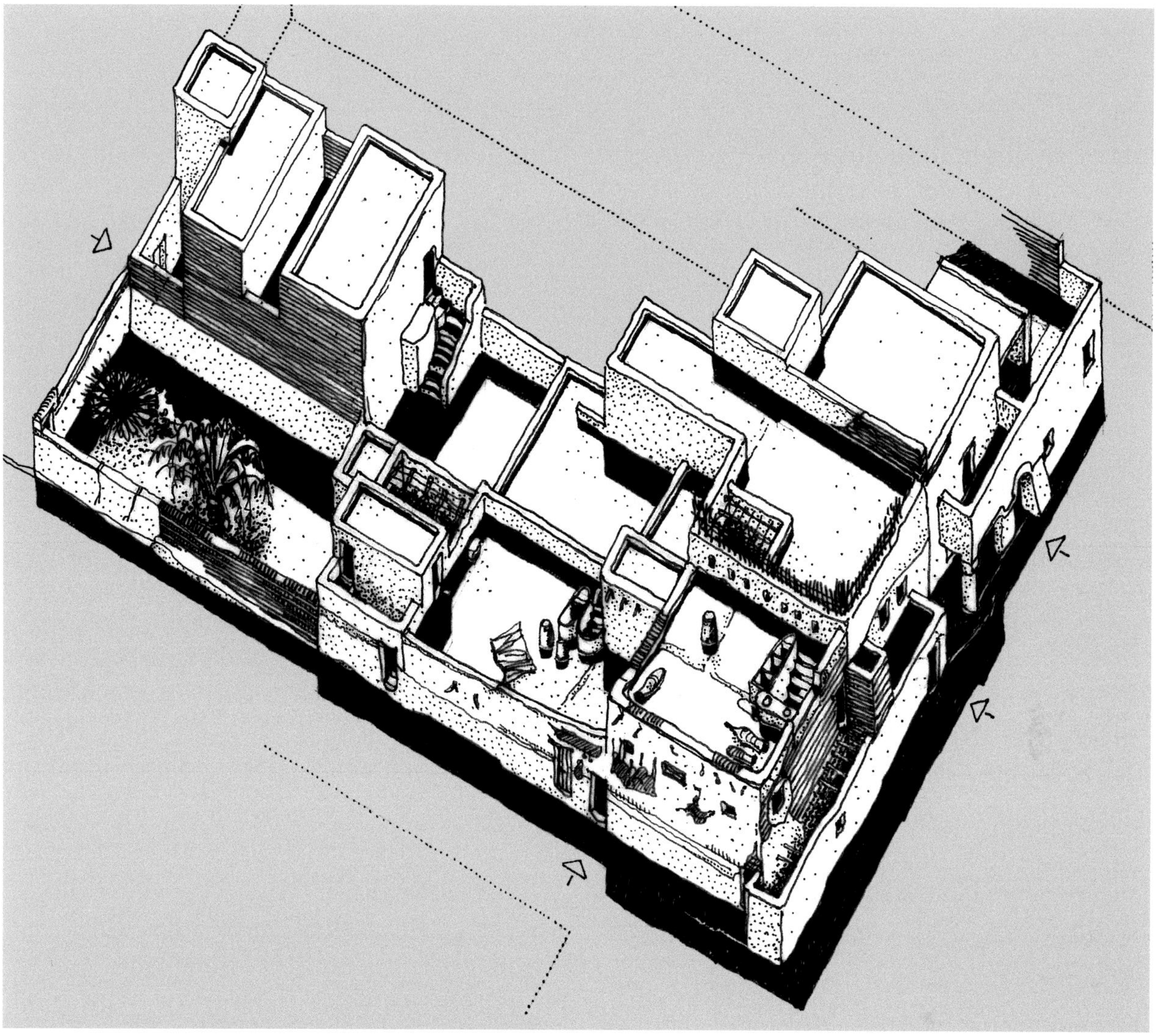

Figure 49. Look at the roof terraces of house 1 and adjacent dwellings in Bashendi

Figure 50. House 1, view from the women's reception room towards the reception room

Figure 51. House 1, kitchen

Figure 52. House 1, the toilet on the roof terrace with an exit to the street

Figure 53. House 1, storage bins on the roof

IV.2 - House 2 in Bashendi

This house forms part of the ancient nucleus of the *ezba*, in which three houses open onto a communal courtyard (Figure 55). It is likely that these three households formed part of the same family, as is common in this situation. The semi-public space is connected via a covered alleyway with the western edge of the village.

The plastered and whitewashed lower walls of the

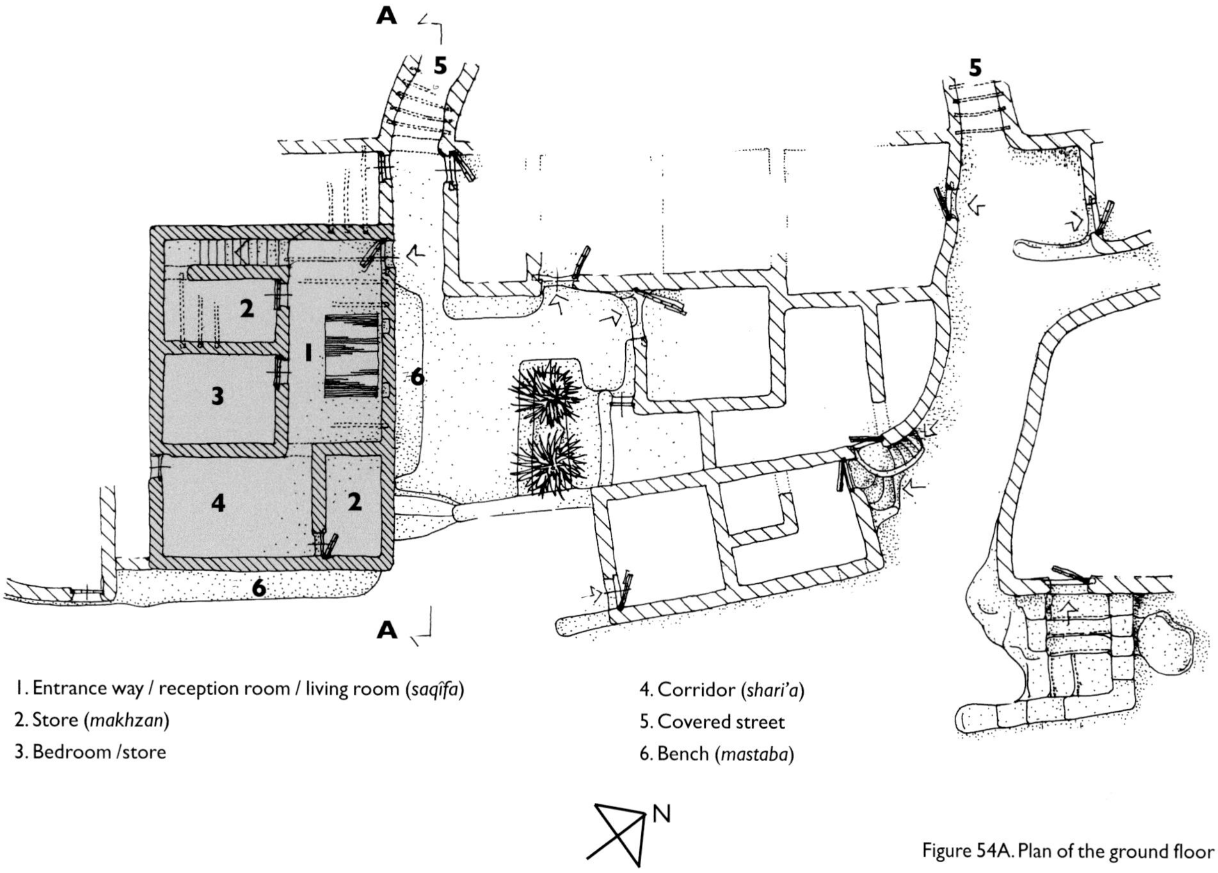

1. Entrance way / reception room / living room (*saqifa*)
2. Store (*makhzan*)
3. Bedroom /store
4. Corridor (*shari'a*)
5. Covered street
6. Bench (*mastaba*)

Figure 54A. Plan of the ground floor

Figure 54B. Elevation of the south-east façade

Figure 54C. North-east façade (profile A-A)

Figure 54. House 2 in Bashendi, plans and elevations

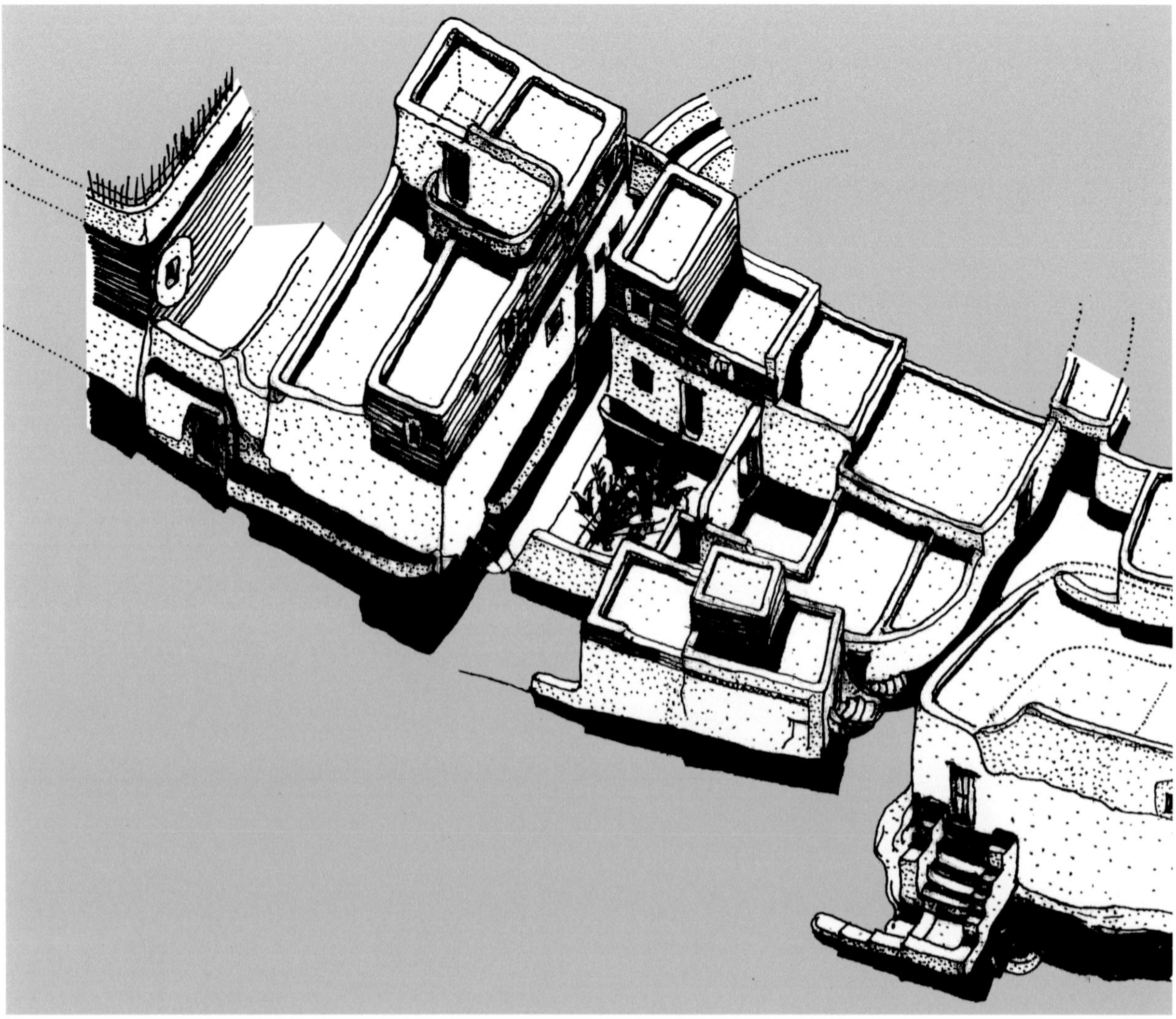

Figure 55. House 2, part of the ancient nucleus of the *ezba* Bashendi

Figure 56. South-west façade of house 2 in Bashendi

Figure 57. Bashendi, entrance of a neighbouring house

Figure 58. Bashendi, communal courtyard and covered alleyway

Figure 59. South-east façade of house 2 in Bashendi

façade have been extended to long benches (*mastabas*) at several locations. The transition to the earthen coloured masonry of the upper storey is in this case marked by a band of decorative open brickwork (Figures 58-59).

IV.3 - A house in Balât

The house chosen for this documentation is abandoned, but this happened only recently so the internal divisions and the use of the various rooms can still be made out clearly. The fixed elements of furniture are still intact. The frontal section of the neighbouring house to the left seems to have been related to the house, possibly as a guest house. This relationship is demonstrated by various openings in the wall dividing the houses.

The neighbouring house on the right, which partly extends over the street, has likewise been abandoned and is showing signs of neglect. The roof of the upper storey has collapsed entirely.

Next to the entrance of the house is a storage space or the like, which perhaps also served as a guest reception room (*maq'ad*). The living room (*saqîfa*) follows next, with the equipment for a winter kitchen. Behind this room lies the female domain around the patio kitchen containing the bread oven (similar to Eigner 1984, figure 24). The upper storey contains another kitchen (Figure 66), for use in the summer months, with a side-chamber, a washing area, and living quarters (*mijlis*). It is remarkable that the house has no toilet facility.

The concentric arrangement of the rooms from intimate to public has appeared clearly from the study of this house. The difference in living quarters for the summer and the winter are also obvious. In this case, however, the separation of the spaces into male and female quarters is less strictly applied. From the arrangement of the rooms, it is clear that the daily practice of life has been reflected in the architecture, so that the cooking place has been placed inside the *saqîfa*, and the roof terrace and its *mijlis* have no internal divisions.

The house seems to have been inhabited by a small family, as also appears from the dimensions of the house, that are notably smaller than that of House I at Bashendi.

The roof is surmounted by a typical rounded fence (Figure 63), as is also visible on the neighbouring houses. This type of fence is made of palm ribs set in clay, the ribs protruding above the edge of the clay moulding. This type of fence determines the village sky line in Dakhleh.

The entrance to the house has an elaborate façade of a traditional type consisting of a raised arch set within a rectangle of decorative brickwork (Figure 62). Three ceramic plates are set in this composition. The patterns of the brickwork have all but disappeared beneath the later plastering of the lower walls and around the window openings. The edge of the roof is ruinous.

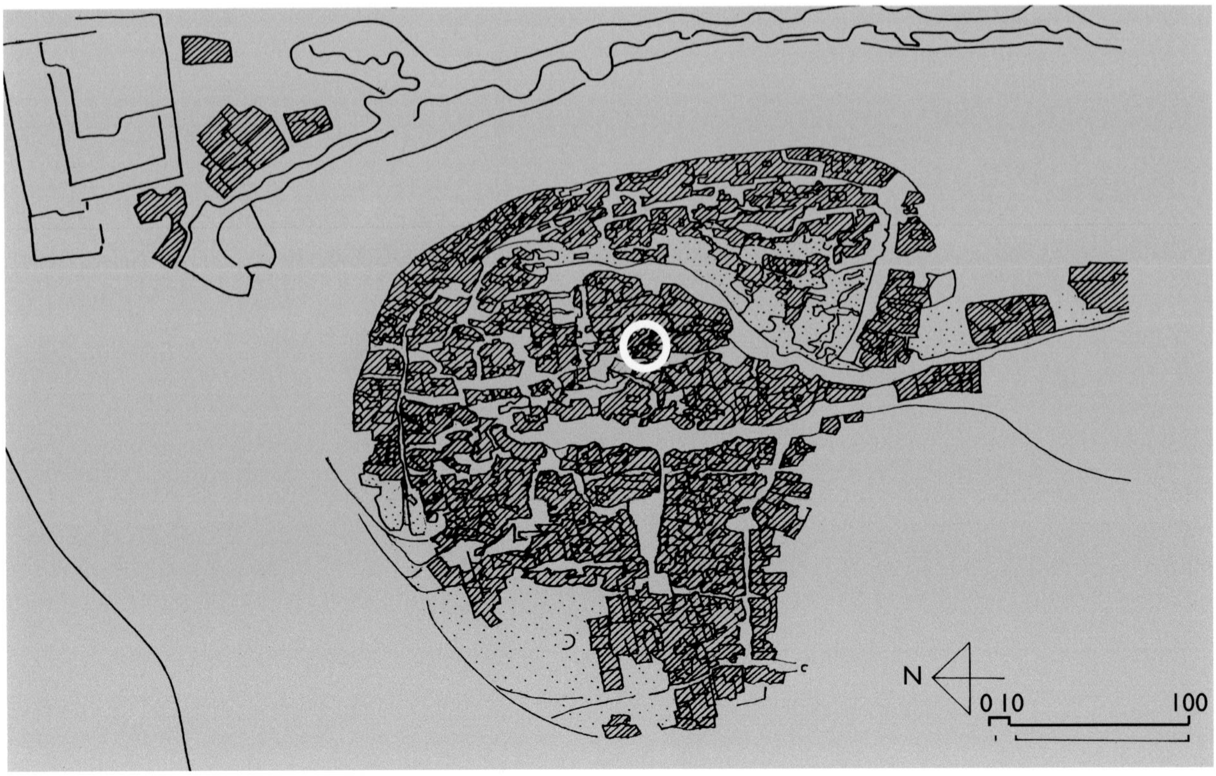

Figure 60. Schematic plan of Balât with the location of the house

Figure 61A. Elevation of the south-west façade (CC)

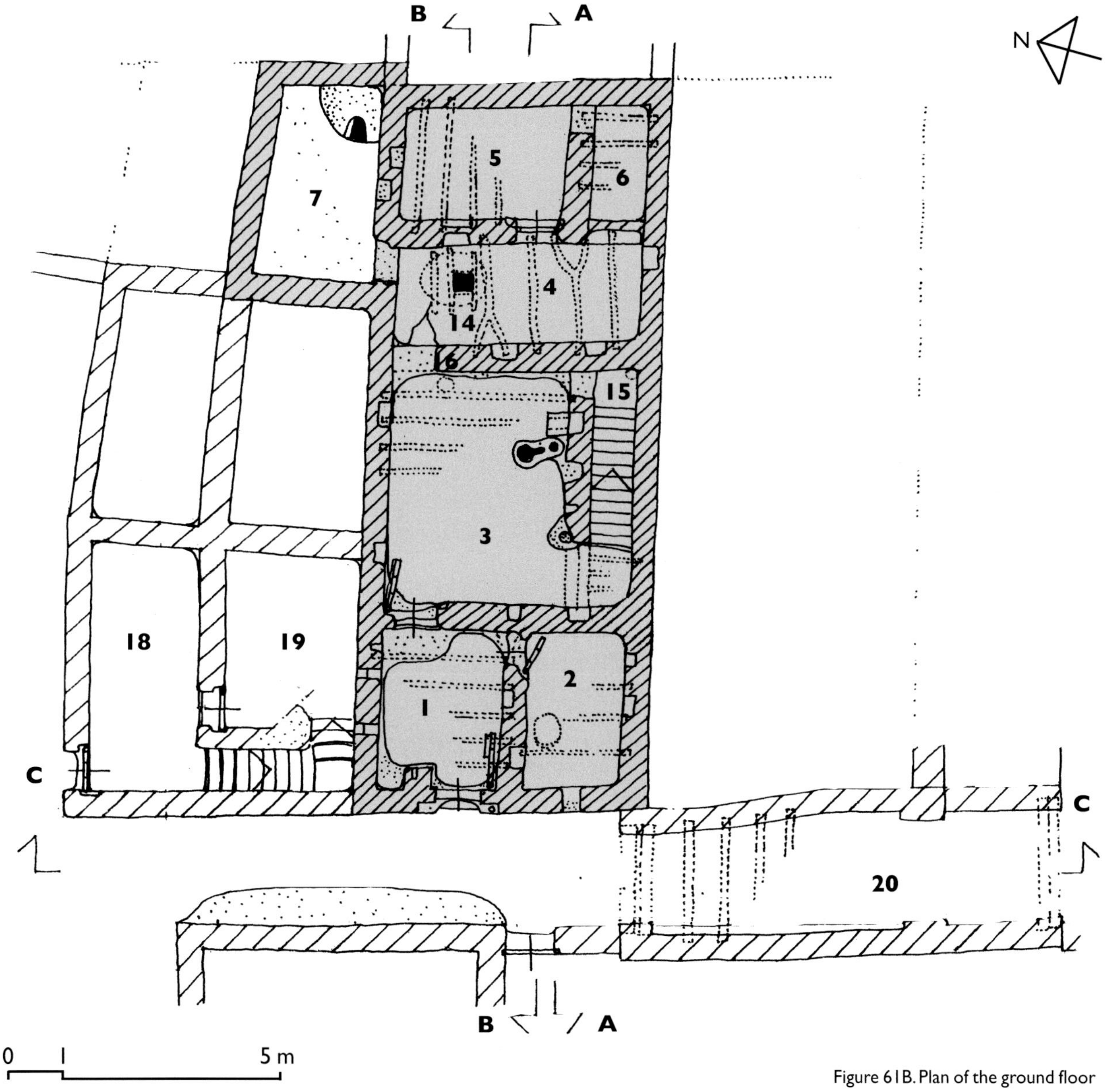

Figure 61B. Plan of the ground floor

Figure 61. House in Balât, plans and elevations

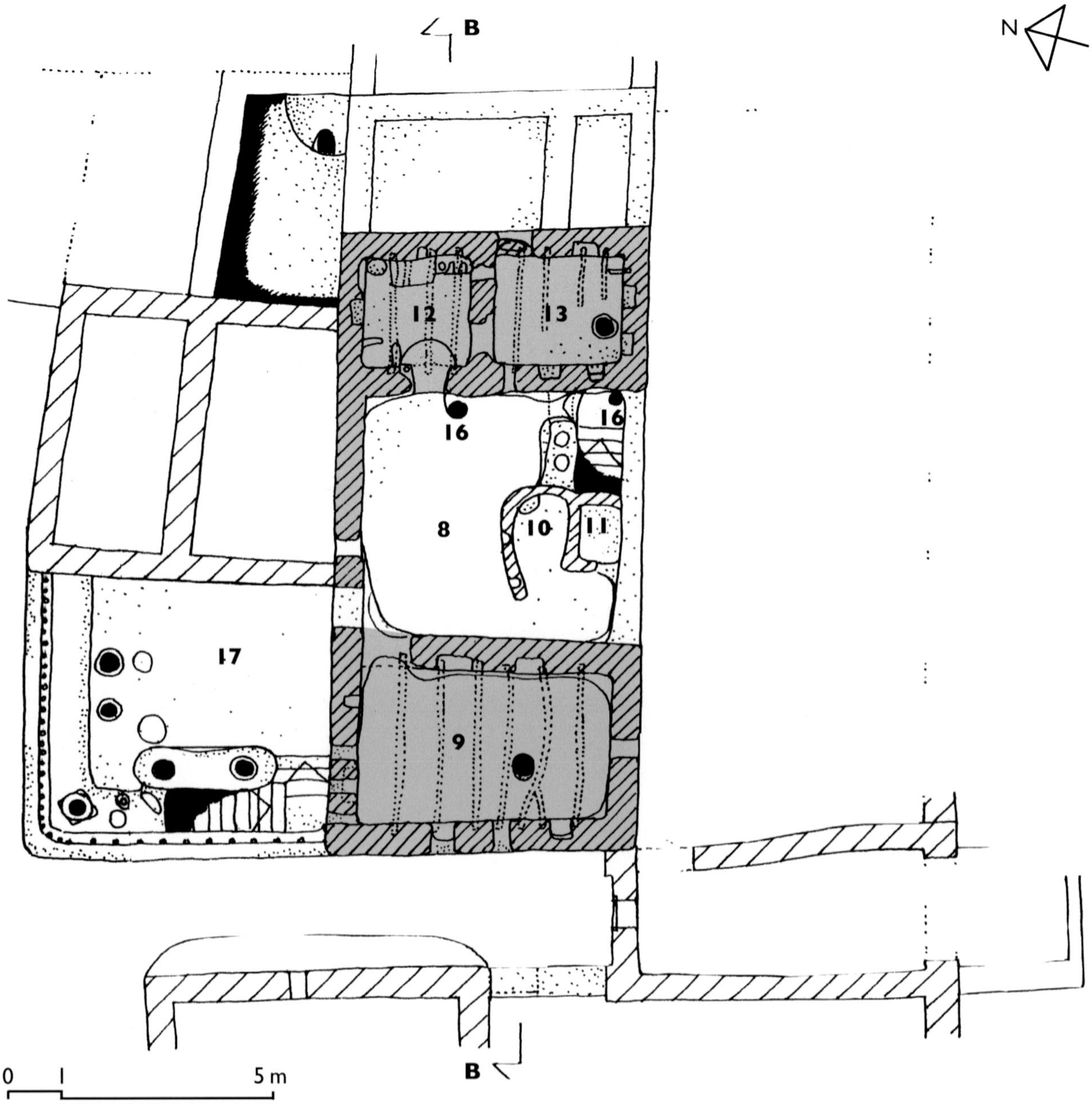

Figure 61C. Plan of the first floor

1. Entrance way
2. Store (*makhzan*)
3. Reception room / living room (*saqîfa*) and winter kitchen
4. Hall (*shari'a*)
5. Bedroom
6. Bathroom (*hammâm*)
7. Kitchen (*matbakh*) with bread oven
8. Roof terrace
9. Upstairs living room (*mijlis*)
10. Laundry yard
11. Chicken pen (*katakît*)
12. Summer kitchen
13. Scullery plan of the first floor
14. Underground store
15. Cupboard beneath the stairs (*hanût*)
16. Light wells
17. Roof terrace of the neighbouring house
18. Entrance to the neighbouring house (*maq'ad*)
19. Store neighbouring house (*makhzan*)
20. Covered street

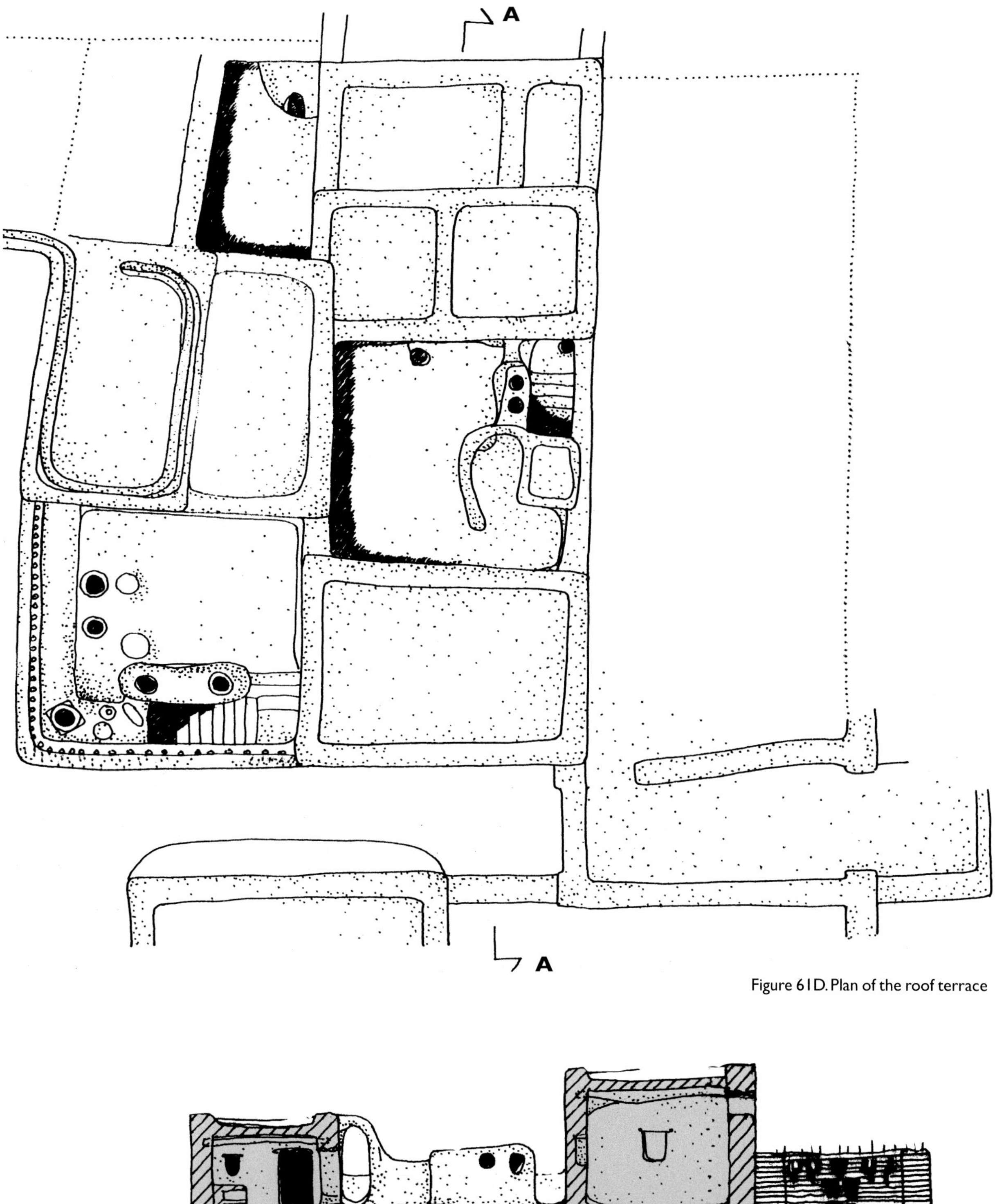

Figure 61D. Plan of the roof terrace

Figure 61E. Section east-west (AA)

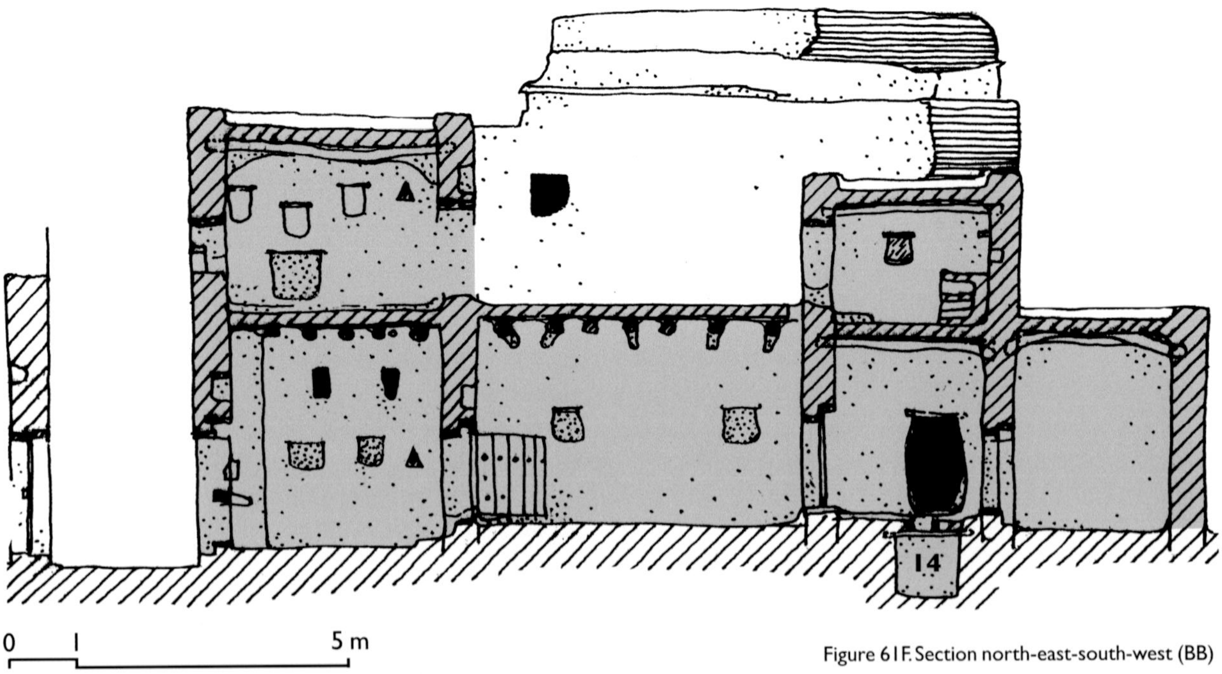

Figure 61F. Section north-east-south-west (BB)

Figure 62. Balât house, decorated entrance in the front façade

Figure 63. Balât house, with typical roof terrace fences

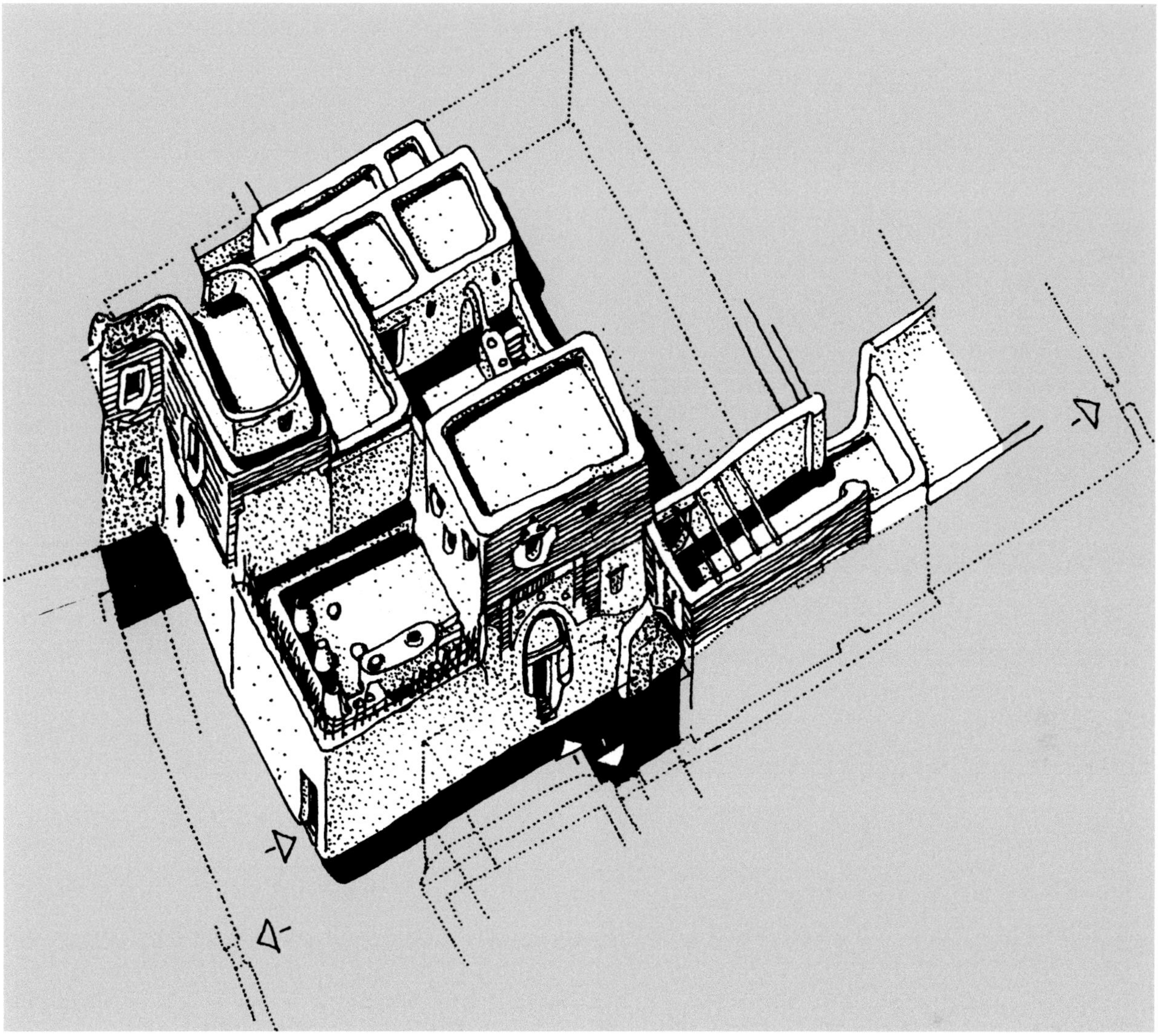

Figure 64. View on the Balât house

Figure 65. Balât house, storage bins on the roof terrace

Figure 66. Balât house, furnishing of the kitchen

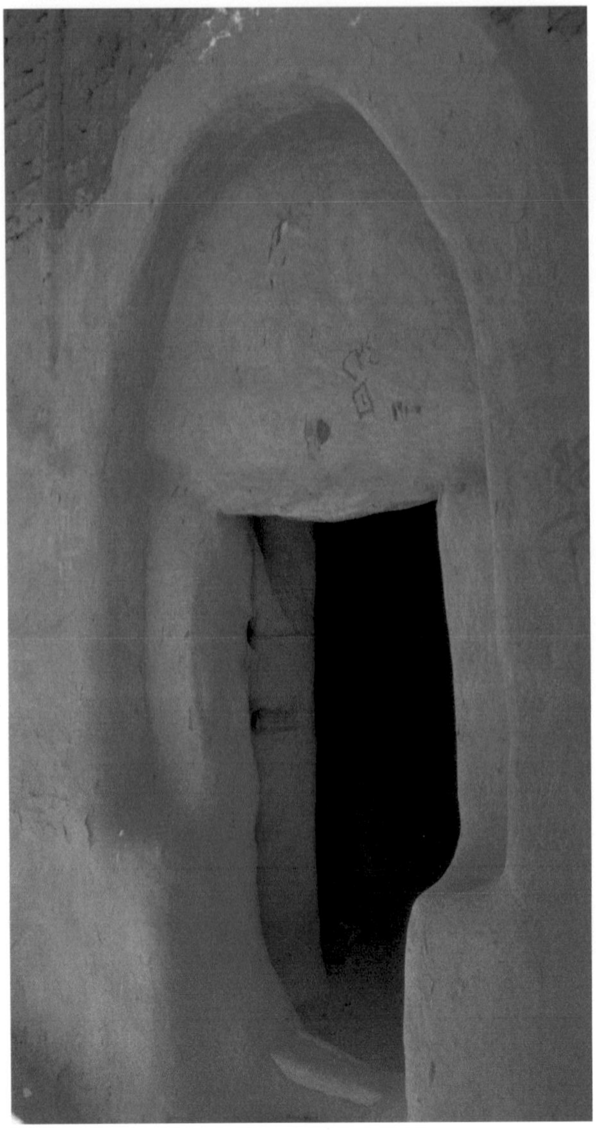

Figure 67. Balât. Entrance of the house

Figure 68. Balât house, the smooth modelled staircase

Chapter V
The D.O.T.A.C.P. Centre

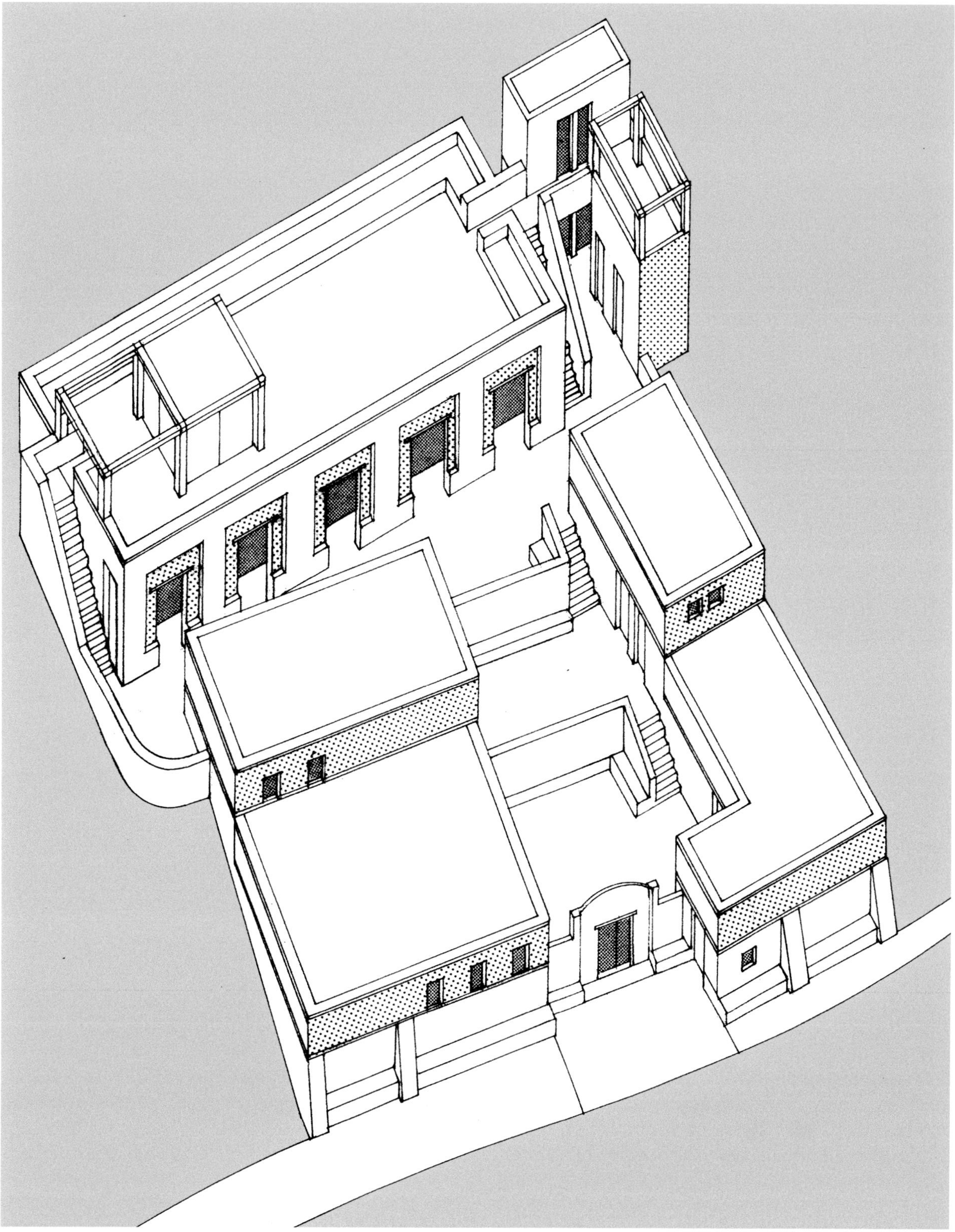

Figure 69. The D.O.T.A.C.P. Centre, projection

The D.O.T.A.C.P. Centre was officially opened on 15 February 1999. It is located on the slope of a hill ("spring mound") beside the road between the village of Sheikh Wali and the town of Mût (Figure 70). It is directed facing a southwestern direction with a view of the palm tree gardens and fields.

The sloping of the hill suggested that the centre should be built in terraces. The building has four main sections that are grouped around three interconnecting courtyards linked with a staircase. The four sections were designed with an eye to their prospective use. The first courtyard behind the entrance to the building contains a

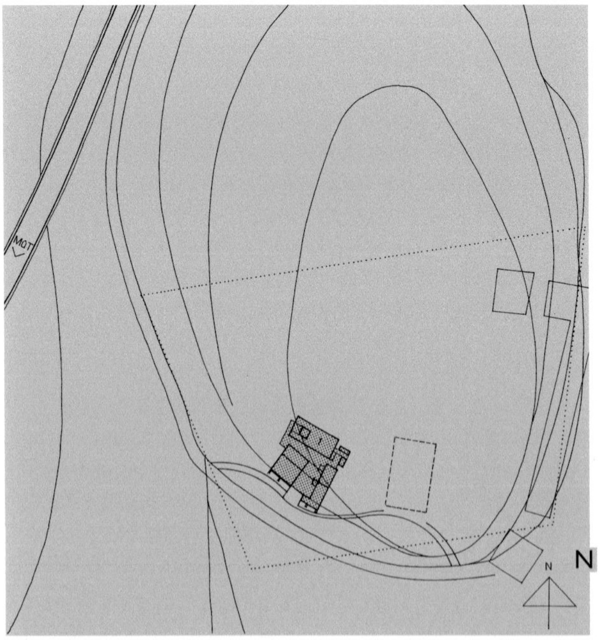

Figure 70. Site plan for the centre

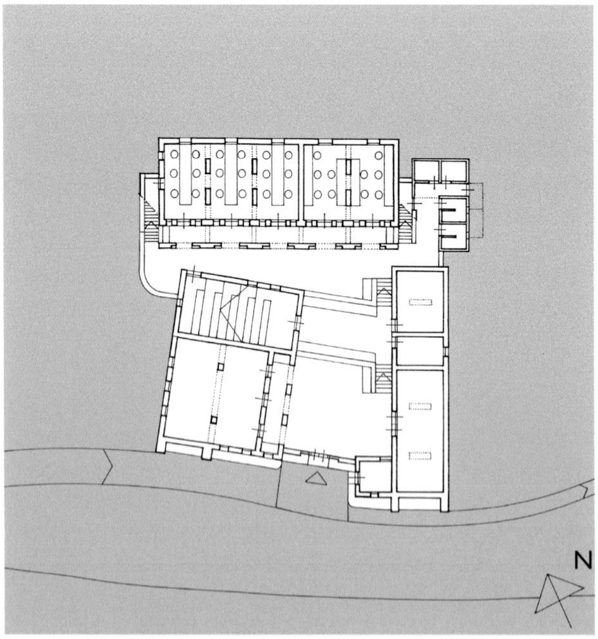

Figure 71. Plan of the ground floor

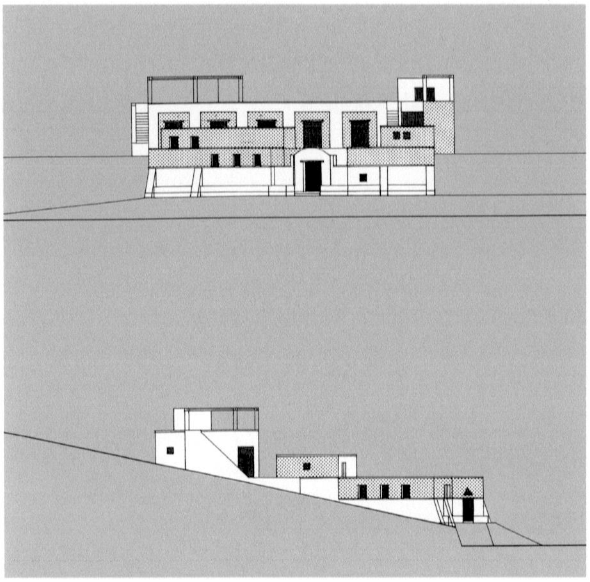

Figure 72. Elevations of the south and west faces

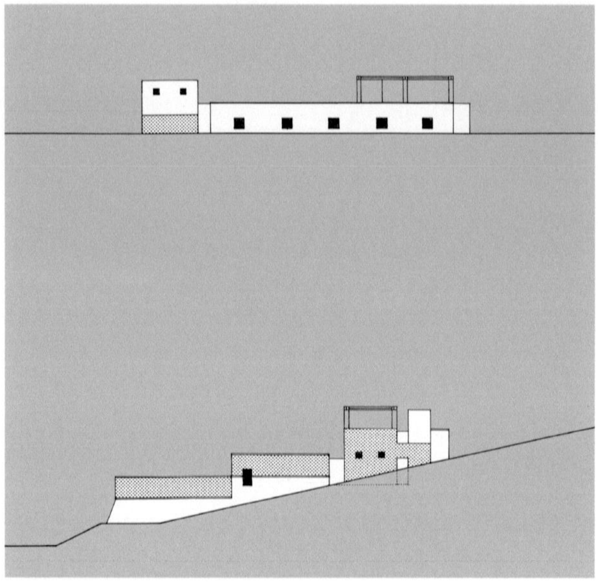

Figure 73. Elevations of the north and east faces

large gathering room with a more or less public role and a storage room for storing fragile materials, which should not be transported through the entire building. A room for the guard is added against the façade of the building. The second courtyard is smaller. It contains a classroom and a small kitchen and another storage room. The highest level of the building comprises an elongated court enclosed by a row of workrooms and laboratories. The southeastern corner of the building contains lavatories and a shower. The roof terrace on the laboratories can also be used, for instance as a drawing studio.

The shape of the building has been made to refer to local types. A characteristic element of the local architecture is the assemblage of roughly cubic components built in mud brick into one complex whole. Usually, these assembled shapes have grown over time. The present building has been inspired by this process.

The mud brick walls have been constructed with a thickness of 40 cm, which is the common size for bearing walls in the oasis. The windows have been kept small. The roofs are flat, constructed of wooden beams with a palm rib covering and a layer of plastered mud.

The only part of the building constructed in stone, burned brick and cement is the lavatory unit. The foundations and the lowest courses of the walls of the entire building have been constructed out of limestone blocks brought in from the Nile Valley to provide more stability.

Figure 74. The newly finished centre, west view

Figure 75. The entrance of the centre

Figure 76. The lower courtyards seen from the roof of the upper terrace

The advantages of building in mud brick are maintained, in that the thick walls provide an excellent isolation of the inner room temperature. The location of the windows provides cross ventilation of the spaces.

In front of the gathering hall of the lower terrace and the laboratories and workrooms of the upper terrace verandas have been added to provide shade against overheating of the doorways. The walls of the courtyards are provided with long benches of mudbrick (*mastabas*). The façade of the building is decorated with a series of pilasters inspired by some local houses.

The entire surface of the walls has been plastered with a mud plastering, which has been whitewashed on the interior.

The erection of the centre was completely carried out by a local builder under the direction of A.J. Mills. A number of minor details have had to be adjusted during the course of the building process, but on the whole the building was erected in accordance with its original concept. It is to be hoped that the presence of this building in the heart of the oasis will in itself already have a beneficial influence on the status of mudbrick architecture in Dakhleh. It will certainly form a suitable housing for the teaching of courses in local history, conservation and archaeology of the Dakhleh Oasis as provided by the D.O.T.A.C.P.

Bibliography

Almásy, L.E., 1997. *Schwimmer in der Wüste: Auf der Suche nach der Oase Zarzura,* Neuauflage des Werks: Unbekannte Sahara von 1939, second edition. Innsbruck.

Aufrère, S., Goyon, J.-C., Golvin, J.-C., 1994. *l'Egypte restituée*, II. Paris.

Badawy, A., 1966. *Architecture in Ancient Egypt and the Near East.* Cambridge.

Badawy, A., 1968. *A History of Egyptian Architecture: The Empire.* Berkeley.

Bagnall, R.S. (ed.), 1997. *The Kellis Agricultural Account Book*, Dakhleh Oasis Project Monograph 7. Oxford.

el-Banna, S., 1967. *Einfluss des Klimas auf den Wohnungs- und Städtebau in ariden Klimaten*, diss. Hannover.

Beadnell, H.J.L., 1901. *Dakhla Oasis: Its Topography and Geology,* Survey Department, Geological Survey Report; 4. Cairo.

Bianca, S., 1975. *Architektur und Lebensform im islamischen Stadtwesen.* Zurich.

Bourdieu, P., 1970. "The Berber House or the World Reversed", *Social Sciences Information* 9,2 (1970), 151-170.

Broadbent, G., 1990. *Emerging Concepts in Urban Space Design.* New York.

Churcher, C.S. and Mills, A.J. (eds), 1999. *Reports from the Survey of Dalehleh Oasis, Western Desert of Egypt*, Dakhleh Oasis Project Monograph 2. Oxford.

Clarke, S., & Engelbach, R., 1930. *Ancient Egyptian Masonry: The Building Craft.* New York.

Davies, N. de G., 1929. "The Town House in Ancient Egypt", *Metropolitan Museum Studies* 1, 231-55.

Décobert, C., 1969. "Notes sur le site d'al-Qasaba (oasis de Dakhla)", *Annales Islamologiques* 15, 473-93.

Décobert, C., 1982. "Un espace-prétexte: les oasis d'Egypte vues par les géographes arabes", *Studia Islamica* 55, 95-114.

Décobert, C., & Gril, D., 1981. *Linteaux a épigraphes de l'oasis de Dakhla,* Supplément aux Annales Islamologiques 1. Cairo.

Desroches, C., 1938. "Un modèle de maison citadine du Nouvel Empire (Musée du Louvre: no. E.5357)", *Revue d'Egyptologie* 3, 17-25, pl. I-II.

Donnadieu, C.P. and Didillon, H.J., 1977. *Habiter le désert : les maisons mozabites, recherches sur un type d'architecture traditionelle pré-saharienne.* Brussels.

Drovetti, B., 1821. "Journal d'un voyage a la vallée de Dakel, vers la fin de 1818", in: Jomard, E.F. (ed.), *Voyage a l'Oasis de Thèbes et dans les déserts situés a l'orient et a l'occident de la Thébaïde.* Paris.

Egli, E., 1951. *Die neue Stadt in Landschaft und Klima: Climate and Town Districts - Consequences and Demands,* Zurich.

Egypt's Golden Age: The Art of Living in the New Kingdom 1558-1085 B.C., (exhibition catalogue). Boston, 1982.

Eigner, D., 1984. *Ländliche Architektur und Siedlungsformen im Ägypten der Gegenwart.* Wien.

Endruweit, A., 1989. "Die Wohnhäuser in Amarna: Zur architektonischen Resonanz auf die Erfordernisse eines Wüstenklimas", *Göttinger Miszellen* 112, 11-22.

Endruweit, A., 1994. *Städtischer Wohnbau in Ägypten: Klimagerechte Lehmarchitektur in Amarna.* Berlin.

Evans-Pritchard, E.E., 1949. *The Sanusi of Cyrenaica.* Oxford.

Fakhry, A., 1973. *The Oases of Egypt I, Siwa Oasis.* Cairo.

Fathy, H., 1973. *Architecture for the Poor.* Cairo.

Gayraud, R.-P., & Décobert, C., 1982. "Les fouilles islamiques d'al-Qasaba (Oasis de Dakhla)", *Annales Islamologiques* 18, 273-86.

Giddy, L.L., 1987. *Egyptian Oases: Bahariya, Dakhla, Farafra and Kharga during Pharaonic Times.* Warminster.

Grossmann, P., 1989. "Some Observations on the late Roman Necropolis of al-Bagawat", in: Fakhry, A., *The Egyptian Desert: The Tombs of Al-Bagawat in the Kharga Oasis.* Cairo.

el-Hakim, O., 1993. *Nubian Architecture: The Egyptian Vernacular Experience.* Cairo.

Hivernel, J., 1996. *Balat: étude ethnologique d'une communauté rurale.* Bibliothèque d'Etude 113. Cairo.

Hölscher, U., 1954. *The Excavations of Medinet Habu V: Post-Ramesside Remains.* Chicago.

Husson, G., 1983. *OIKIA: Le vocabulaire de la maison privée en Egypte d'apres les papyrus grecs.* Paris.

Kaper, O.E., 1997. *Temples and gods in Roman Dakhleh: Studies in the Indigenous Cults of an Egyptian Oasis.* Groningen.

Khouri-Haddad, Y.P., 1966. *Architecture and Climate in Rural Egypt.* Ann Arbor.

Kila, J.D., 1994. *Adobe or Mudbrick Architecture; history and Conservation Problems.* Leiden.

Harding King, W.J., 1925. *Mysteries of the Libyan Desert: A Record of Three Years of Exploration in the Heart of that Vast & Waterless Region.* London.

Leclant, J., 1993. "Oasis Histoire d'un mot", in: *A la croisée des études libyco-berbères mélanges offerts à P.*

Galand-Pernet et L. Galand. Paris.

Mills, A.J., 1982. "The Dakhleh Oasis Project: A Report on the First Two Seasons", *Annales du Service des Antiquités de l'Egypte* 68, 71-78.

Mills, A.J., 1979. "Dakhleh Oasis Project: Report on the First Season of Survey (October-December 1978), *Journal of the Society for the Study of Egyptian Antiquities* 9, 163-85.

Mills, A.J., 1993. "The Dakhleh Oasis Columbarium Farmhouse", *Bulletin de la Société Archéologique d'Alexandrie* 45, 193-198.

Mitwalli, M., 1943. "The Population of the Egyptian Oases", *Bulletin de la Société Royale de Géographie d'Egypte* XXI, 289-312.

Moritz, B., 1900. "Excursion aux oasis du désert libyque", *Bulletin de la Société khédiviale de Géographie*, 5e Série, 8, 429-475.

Osing, J., 1986. "Einige Notizen zu den Oasen", *Göttinger Miszellen* 89, 70-72.

Osing, J., Moursi, M., Arnold, Do., Neugebauer, O., Parker R.A., Nur el-Din, M.A., 1982. *Denkmäler der Oase Dachla aus dem Nachlass von Ahmed Fakhry*, Archäologische Veröffentlichungen des Deutschen Archäologischen Instituts, Abt. Kairo; 28. Mainz.

Richter, L., 1960. *Islands of the Sahara: Through the Oases of Libya*. Leipzig.

Ricke, H., 1932. *Der Grundriß des Amarna-Wohnhauses*. Leipzig.

Ricke, H., 1966. "Ein Hausmodell im Kestnermuseum zu Hannover", *Zeitschrift für Ägyptische Sprache und Altertumskunde* 93, 119-23.

Schijns, W., 1992. Djenné comme synthèse d'une conception spatiale architectonique, in: Maas, P., Mommersteeg, G., *Djenné chef-d'œuvre architectural*. Eindhoven.

Sers, J.-F., 1994. *Sous la direction de Théodore Monod: Désert libyque*. Paris.

Spencer, A.J., 1979. *Brick Architecture in Ancient Egypt*. Warminster.

Steele, J., 1988. *Hassan Fathy*. London.

Steele, J., 1997. *An Architecture for People: The Complete Works of Hassan Fathy*. London and Cairo.

Timm, S., 1992. *Das christlich-koptische Ägypten in arabischer Zeit* VI. Wiesbaden.

Vycichl, W., 1983. *Dictionnaire étymologique de la langue copte*. Leuven.

Wagner, G., 1987. *Les oasis d'Egypte a l'époque grecque, romaine et byzantine d'apres les documents grecs*, Bibliothèque d'Etude 100. Cairo.

Wilkinson, J.G., 1843. *Modern Egypt and Thebes: Being a Description of Egypt II*.

Winlock, H.E. (ed.), 1936. *Dakhleh Oasis: Journal of a Camel Trip made in 1908*, The Metropolitan Museum of Art, Department of Egyptian Art, 5. New York.

Woodforde, J., 1976. *Bricks to build a house*. London.

Worp, K.A., 1995. *Greek Papyri from Kellis I*, Dakhleh Oasis Project Monograph 3. Oxford.